North Melbourne Tel: 01245 442292	8/16	

Please return this book on or before the date shown above. To renew go to www.essex.gov.uk/libraries, ring 0345 603 7628 or go to any Essex library.

Essex County Council

D1426672

Easy Indian Super Meals

ZAINAB JAGOT AHMED

Dedicated to my beautiful little princess ... Aaliyah

Easy Indian
Super Meals

for babies, toddlers and the family

ZAINAB JAGOT AHMED

EBURY
PRESS

Contents

Introduction

Every parent wants to feed their baby nutritious food to ensure their little one has the best start in life. So, being a new mum, I was extremely cautious about the types of food I was feeding my daughter, Aaliyah, when I began weaning her at 6 months. A feeling I'm sure every woman can relate to at some point during her career as 'mum'.

After reading books, numerous websites, and seeking advice from family and friends about weaning and the best weaning foods, my anxiety about "where to begin?!" settled, and Aaliyah's solid food journey began. I started with iron-fortified baby rice (with her usual milk), and puréed fruit and vegetables combined with her regular milk feeds. That seemed straightforward enough. However, only a month later when Aaliyah turned 7 months old, she was already set for Stage 2 feeding (soft lumps, new tastes, flavours and textures). The confusion and panic of "what should I feed her now?!" started all over again! Buying bland, processed, lumpy baby food was not appealing in the slightest! Particularly as the more processed the food, the more additives it contains which ultimately means the nutritional content is reduced.

I completely understand how tempting it is to buy processed baby food if you are a busy parent, and it is fine occasionally, but feeding your little one nutritionally inadequate food will be detrimental to health, as babies need nutrient-rich food for healthy growth.

As parents we also have a responsibility to shape and maintain healthy eating habits as early as possible, so our little ones develop a positive relationship with healthy foods. The idea here is that if children are exposed to nutritious meals daily as they grow, this will help to create healthy lifelong habits assisting weight control. As you know, obesity is a long-term, ongoing issue in the UK so we need to do our best to curb it, not just for society, but for our kids too! Being an overweight or obese child at school can't be fun. Teasing and bullying can cause low self-esteem and depression. Later in life, there are additional health problems to consider – diabetes, heart disease, high blood pressure and joint problems. So it's important to act now as obese children are increasingly likely to grow into obese adults.

Therefore, home-cooking was the obvious choice for me because I could cook with nutrient-rich foods and know exactly what ingredients were going into Aaliyah's meals. It would be more cost-effective, fresher, healthier and tastier. By planning ahead, I could also cook and freeze meals for the forthcoming week, saving valuable time too.

So Aaliyah's Stage 2 feeding began with steamed vegetables and cheese all blended to a soft lumpy consistency. But then I thought, "why am I feeding my daughter such bland food?" Being a British Asian, I wasn't raised on steamed veggies and cheese and neither are billions of other people across the world!

Wanting Aaliyah to be in touch with her roots, I searched for Indian-influenced baby food recipes online and for any cookery books I could buy, but surprisingly I didn't find much. I also asked family and friends if they knew of any good Indian baby food cookery books, and they didn't know of any either. We were all in the same boat! One day, deep in thought I felt a flicker of inspiration and then 'PING!'... light bulb moment! I decided to create my own healthy adaptations of traditional Indian recipes.

My first attempt was Gajar Halwa (carrot dessert), simply because the main ingredient is carrot, a very tasty sweet root vegetable which is extremely healthy for babies. I cooked up a batch following a conventional recipe but stripped it right back to remove all the bad stuff. I avoided overcooking the carrots as some recipes suggest, maintaining their moisture and natural sweetness, and the sugar was replaced with raisins. I served it up to my daughter and SUCCESS! Her little eyes lit up with delight after the first mouthful as though it was her first trip to a sweet shop, she wanted more and more. Then suddenly 'PING!'... another light bulb moment! I thought "WOW, she loved it! I'm going to write an Indian-inspired baby and toddler food cookery book!"

After the success of this recipe, I spent a period of months researching and detailing the health benefits of culinary spices, also known as **'Super Spices'**, food groups and **'Super Foods'**, to ensure I provided Aaliyah with all of the vitamins and minerals she needed for healthy growth and development. After collating this information, I experienced yet another light bulb moment and came up with the concept of creating 'Super Meals' for babies, toddlers and the whole family. So that my fellow mummy is the story of how this book came to be.

What are 'Super Meals'?

The 'Super' of Super Meals refers to the extra health benefits associated with these meals over and above normal meals, due to the inclusion of carefully selected foods, Super Foods and Super Spices. When fused together they produce scrumptious meals chock-full with nutritional value for babies and toddlers. In other words:

Regular Foods
+ Super Foods
+ Super Spices
= Super Meals

I've used my 'Banana and Cinnamon Roti Wrap' recipe (page 95), as an example of how Super Meals work in this cookery book:

Roti (Regular Food)
+ Banana (Super Food)
+ Cinnamon (Super Spice)
= Roti Wrap (Super Meal)

The roti (Indian flatbread or chapatti) fulfils the basic starchy food requirement to provide much-needed energy for baby; the banana, an excellent high-energy fruit provides potassium vital for heart function, healthy muscle growth and helps the body to absorb calcium; the cinnamon contributes towards a healthy immune system, is great for digestion and brain function, as well as offering a warm fragrant sweetness. All of these health benefits are wrapped up into one tasty snack that your little one will wholeheartedly munch on. So you can rest assured, I have created some cracking recipes that are **delicious, powerful, energy-packed, well-balanced Super Meals**, boosting the antioxidant levels on your little one's colourful plastic plate.

Who is this Book For?

Easy Indian Super Meals is a useful culinary guide for any parent looking to ditch the bland baby food and move on to yummy adventurous baby food: expectant mums for future reference, and new or existing parents who want to try something a bit different with their second, third or fourth child.

It is also for parents interested in learning about safely introducing aromatic spices into their little one's diet, the spices that are safe for baby, the health benefits of super spices and super foods, and the nutritional requirements for baby and the rest of the family. Making Easy Indian Super Meals a handy reference guide for years to come.

How this Book Works

Instead of separating this book by feeding stage, I have separated the chapters by meal type – veggie, fish, finger food, sweet, meat and so on. I've done this to make it easier for busy parents to find the type of recipes they are looking for quickly, particularly for parents wanting to pass specific dietary requirements on to their baby, for example raising baby as a vegetarian. All of these chapters, however, include stage 2 and stage 3 recipes. They are written in the top corner of each page for ease. I've also included some of my own personal experiences of weaning my daughter at the beginning of each chapter. I'm hoping you will find them useful, from one parent to another.

If you are looking for the official nutritional advice, all of the details can be found in the first few chapters before the recipes begin.

They includes details on milk feeds for baby, number of meals per day, food groups, super foods, vitamins and minerals, health benefits of spices, how to introduce spices to baby safely and so on.

As your little one progresses on to Stage 4: 1–3 Years recipes, toddlers can eat pretty much everything. For this reason, all vegetarian, meat and fish meals are under the same chapter but are all clearly labelled for convenience.

And finally, as your little one moves into the school years (3 years plus), there's a handy chapter at the end of this book focussed on preparing quick, tasty meals for kids – all meals ready in 15 minutes or less.

Throughout this book baby is referred to as 'she'. The only reason for this is that I have a daughter, so for me it's the obvious choice.

Feeding Stages

There are many feeding stages a baby needs to progress through before she is ready for the big table. While stage 1 from 4–6 months involves first tastes and purées, if you're reading this book I'm guessing you've already sailed through this stage and are looking for some more exciting meals to feed your baby. So the feeding stages included in this book start from 7 months and go all the way through to family meals and quick after-school meals, giving you meal inspiration for years to come!

Stage 2 – 7 Months Plus: weaning babies ready for new textures, soft lumps, new tastes and new flavours, by introducing tiny amounts of aromatic spices to tempt curious little taste buds. Self-feeding also begins.

Stage 3 – 10 Months Plus: older babies ready to progress to the next level of spice for more flavoursome meals. Meals are chunkier consisting of chopped food instead of mashed. Self-feeding continues.

Stage 4 – 1–3 Years Plus: spice training complete. Toddlers are ready for family meals with some small changes.

The School Years – 3–5 Years Plus: pre-schoolers and older school children needing quick, tasty nutritious meals to satisfy hunger pangs after a busy day at school.

Feel free to use these feeding stages as loose guidelines. As your baby grows you'll notice the stages will blur into the next. So it's a good idea to adapt some of my recipes to your baby's palate. For example, Aaliyah had lots of favourite recipes in stage 2 weaning but after a couple of months she was ready for chunkier stage 3 meals.

I didn't, however, want to stop feeding her her favourite meals because she was ready to move on. I adapted the recipe to suit her feeding stage by simply increasing the level of spice in my stage 2 recipes to reflect that of stage 3. So ¼ teaspoon of garlic was increased to ½ teaspoon or even 1 teaspoon, while following the same recipe. I also kept the meals chunkier and served her favourite curries with accompaniments such as soft mushy rice, roti or pitta bread pieces and protein-rich quinoa to make the meals more filling. This worked really well as it meant Aaliyah could enjoy her stage 2 recipes for a little longer.

IMPORTANT: do not feed your little one any recipes earlier than their recommended start age.

So it's fine to 'spice up', as your baby's palate will already be used to a little more spice, but not necessarily the other way around.

Cooking Technique

In my family, traditional Indian home-cooking (more often than not) involves throwing all of the ingredients in the same pot to bubble away until tender – spices, vegetables and meat.

While this is great for one-pot meals (less dishes to wash!), it does mean that some of the nutrients can be lost from over-cooking the vegetables. This is something I was particularly conscious of, especially when I was reading about 'feeding your baby a rainbow' of fruits and vegetables and how important it is to maintain these nutrients for baby. So to keep Aaliyah's rainbow bright, I altered my cooking technique to ensure I maintained as many nutrients as possible, steaming the fruits and vegetables separately and adding them to the meal at the end. You'll notice this as you start rustling up some of my recipes.

About the Recipes – No added Salt, Sugar or Chillies!

Choose from yummy vegetable, meat or fish curries, desserts and finger foods as your little one graduates from one feeding stage and on to the next. Some are **traditional Indian recipes with a twist** such as my scrumptious 'Sweet Potato, Apple and Dhal Curry' (page 36). Others are inspired by World cuisine but with an Indian twist, such as my mouth-watering 'Indian Vegetable Paella' (page 59), 'Playdate Pizza Pitta Fingers' (page 96) and a twist on the British classic 'Desi Mac 'n' Cheese with Tuna' (page 73); all guaranteed to leave your little one with a very full and satisfied tummy.

Feeding Baby New Meals – What to Expect

I know how exciting (and also frustrating) offering new meals to baby can be. Enthusiastically I'd cook up a storm in the kitchen and when Aaliyah's meal was ready, I'd put her in her high chair (armed with bib), spoon-feed her her first mouthful and wait for her response; like a contestant on MasterChef waiting for the judge's approval.

In my experience, I found her initial responses to be quite extreme. She either loved her meal, straightaway gobbling up the whole bowlful, or she'd push the food out with her tongue. When she did this I felt really disheartened, thinking "oh no, what if I'm a terrible cook and she can't tell me!"

As time went on, I realised although she appeared not to enjoy some meals, when I offered them to her again either later the same day or another day, she devoured the whole bowl. As she had already experienced the initial taste, both the taste and texture were not a surprise to her anymore.

Now Aaliyah eats almost everything and loves her food, which is great for family meal times and for holidays away from home. In fact, she is very enthusiastic about trying new types of food, which is amazing and a huge relief for me. I like to think in her mind:

food from mummy = yummy food for me to eat

So stay strong and persevere! If your little one rejects some of the meals you have prepared either using your own recipes, or from using recipes in this cookery book, offer the meals again at another time as she may develop a taste for it later, whether it be a week or months' time. In fact, you may have to offer it up to 15 times before she accepts it!

Following the food spitting, turning away from food and spoon pushing, rest assured that all recipes have now been approved and awarded gold stars by my little Princess Aaliyah, and her little friends – the toughest of all food critics.

Super Spices

'Super Spices', although they have been used for medicinal purposes and general well-being across different cultures for generations, is a term awarded to culinary spices by researchers due to their remarkable health-promoting properties and potent antioxidant levels. This is a concept supported by the U.S. Department of Agriculture (USDA). After examining antioxidant activity of specific foods, fruits, vegetables and spices amongst others, they found culinary spices such as cloves, cinnamon and turmeric are bursting with powerful antioxidants. Antioxidants that have an even higher level than some of the more popular Super Foods such as blueberries and avocados, as you'll see in the pyramid on the opposite page.

Consuming antioxidants is massively important for our health to protect our bodies against free radical cell damage. Free radicals are unstable, highly reactive molecules triggered by pollution, pesticides in food, alcohol, smoking and excess fat consumption, causing serious diseases such as heart disease, cancer, strokes, Alzheimer's disease and arthritis later in life.

Super Spices also possess anti-inflammatory properties which protect us from infections, allergies, asthma and more. In fact, research has shown holy basil has anti-inflammatory action comparable to the common painkiller Ibuprofen, and more recently, carvacrol, a plant compound found in oregano is believed to be effective against the infectious winter vomiting bug, the norovirus, offering yet another reason why spices have been awarded with their Super Spice status.

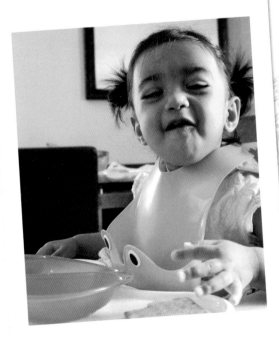

Antioxidant Levels – Super Spices vs Super Foods

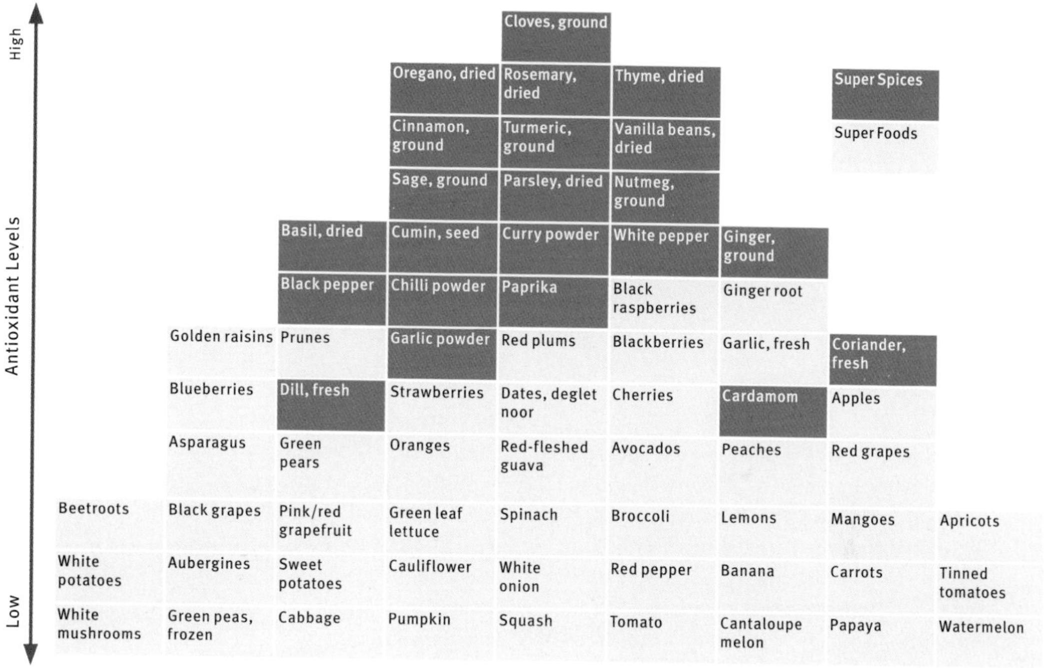

Legend: Super Spices / Super Foods

Antioxidant Levels (vertical axis: High → Low)

				Cloves, ground				
			Oregano, dried	Rosemary, dried	Thyme, dried			
			Cinnamon, ground	Turmeric, ground	Vanilla beans, dried			
			Sage, ground	Parsley, dried	Nutmeg, ground			
		Basil, dried	Cumin, seed	Curry powder	White pepper	Ginger, ground		
		Black pepper	Chilli powder	Paprika	Black raspberries	Ginger root		
	Golden raisins	Prunes	Garlic powder	Red plums	Blackberries	Garlic, fresh	Coriander, fresh	
	Blueberries	Dill, fresh	Strawberries	Dates, deglet noor	Cherries	Cardamom	Apples	
	Asparagus	Green pears	Oranges	Red-fleshed guava	Avocados	Peaches	Red grapes	
Beetroots	Black grapes	Pink/red grapefruit	Green leaf lettuce	Spinach	Broccoli	Lemons	Mangoes	Apricots
White potatoes	Aubergines	Sweet potatoes	Cauliflower	White onion	Red pepper	Banana	Carrots	Tinned tomatoes
White mushrooms	Green peas, frozen	Cabbage	Pumpkin	Squash	Tomato	Cantaloupe melon	Papaya	Watermelon

Adapted from: USDA Database for the Oxygen Radical Absorbance Capacity (ORAC) of Selected Foods, Release 2.

NOTES:

- Fruits and vegetables towards the bottom of the pyramid are still Super Foods, therefore will contain a higher level of nutrients over regular foods.
- This does not represent the entire list of foods within the report. Only the most popular Super Foods have been selected for comparison purposes.
- Further research is underway to determine whether and how Super Spice antioxidant levels benefit human health.

Super Spices in Baby Food – The 'Official' View

Using Indian spices in baby food seems to be a relatively new subject at the moment. There's an abundance of official advice available through the internet, books and health care services focussing on introducing solid food to babies. A great starting point, but official rulebooks mostly ignore the use of aromatic spices in home-cooked baby food. If it is not included in the official advice this doesn't mean you cannot use spices in baby food. It is important to remember these are only recommendations and guidelines. There are no solid procedures you must follow as a parent. So go ahead and throw out the rulebook! You know your baby best, so go with what feels right for you and your little one.

Nevertheless, as the popularity of Indian and exotic baby food grows, attitudes towards using Indian spices are changing, and the fact that the differences are cultural rather than based on scientific findings is coming to the forefront. Being a British Asian, I have both Indian and English culture under my belt, and I can tell you from first-hand experience the difference is entirely cultural. As a child, my mum fed me and my sisters delicious, flavoursome curries with roti and rice from a very young age. This was the first food I ate, even before I was introduced to simple foods like sandwiches when I started school.

Feeding Baby Super Spices – A Good Idea?

Absolutely! Despite the fact research is ongoing to understand exactly if and how the antioxidant levels in Super Spices work to improve health, they do possess a number of other distinct advantages, some of which I will explore now.

Create aromatic, tasty baby food: Our sense of taste and smell are very closely linked. So much so that food would taste bland without our sense of smell. Spices release a delicious aroma when cooked making the food tastier when eaten. A wonderful alternative to adding salt and sugar into baby food, spices will help you create incredibly tasty meals that your little one will wholeheartedly enjoy.

Wider variety of meals: Spices are extremely versatile! Changing one spice in a dish will alter the taste completely. This versatility suggests you can offer a wider variety of meals to your little one. More variety in your little one's diet now will help to keep a fussy eater at bay later. So put the bland food away, and start spicing up that baby food!

Family meal training: If your family meals are already full of flavour, gradually introducing aromatic spices in small amounts will be milder on her little tummy, rather than going from no spice to full spice in one go. This also provides great spice preparation for the big family meals that await her.

Unique health benefits: Each Super Spice has its own unique health benefits that all members of the family can take advantage of. I have outlined the advantages for the core spices I use in my recipes (opposite) so you can see how beneficial spices will be in your little one's diet.

'Super-spicy' breast milk: And finally, did you know if you have been or are currently breastfeeding your little one, she will already have tasted the foods and spices you have been eating? Subtle tastes pass through breast milk and straight into baby's tummy. As spices are already a familiar taste, why not add a pinch of aromatic spices in with her solid food?

Black Pepper: Helps to settle indigestion, constipation and is also good for reducing pain in toothaches.

Cardamom: Prevents cold and flu (influenza), flatulence and throat infections. Also treats asthma, bronchitis, and analgesic properties treat teeth and gums.

Cinnamon: Aids digestion, treats diarrhoea, strengthens the immune system to cure colds, boosts memory and cognitive function, balances blood sugar level (type 2 diabetes) and analgesic properties help to reduce pain in toothaches.

Cloves: Antiseptic properties help fight against colds and flu, bronchitis and athlete's foot. Treats flatulence and boosts memory, digestion and blood circulation. Analgesic properties also reduce pain in toothaches.

Coriander: Aids digestion, treats diarrhoea, provides iron helping to prevent anaemia and protects the skin against eczema and dryness.

Cumin: Supports the development of a healthy immune system, improves oxygen distribution, betters digestion, boosts metabolism and improves the absorption of nutrients.

Paprika: Antibiotic properties help protect against bacterial infections such as tonsillitis, improves blood circulation and aids digestion.

Turmeric: Antibacterial properties help prevent infection in wounds and cuts, aids digestion, boosts immune system function for cold and flu protection, and reduces flatulence and the risk of childhood leukaemia developing.

Which Super Spices are Safe to Use in Baby Food?

Most are safe to use in baby's diet in fresh, ground or dried varieties, provided they are introduced in the correct manner (see How Should I Introduce Super Spices to Baby on page 19). Below is an idea of the aromatic spices you can introduce, although there are more, including chilli powder! Feel free to experiment with them (and others) to uncover new and exciting meals for baby.

When is it Safe to Introduce Super Spices to Baby?

You can introduce single spice additions into your baby's purées from 6 months of age, after first tastes have been accepted. From 7 months, you can start to combine spices to create exciting, delicious meals for your little one. Aaliyah loved all of the different flavours I exposed her palate to. As she grew, she knew when mealtimes were coming. So when I approached her high chair holding her weaning bowl, like a cuddly, angelic seal, she'd clap her hands together with the biggest, gummiest grin on her little face. So gorgeous! She absolutely loved her food, eating all of her meals with gusto.

As with stage 1 weaning, the best time of day to introduce new tastes to your little one is around lunchtime (when baby isn't ravenous but equally isn't sleepy and due a nap). So take advantage of your baby's alertness and curious taste buds by trying new meals then.

If you are cautious or have a known family history of allergies to specific spices, I would recommend waiting 2–3 days before introducing a new spice into your little one's diet. Up to 72 hours should be more than enough time for you to spot any allergic reactions baby might have to certain spices.

While allergic reactions to spices are uncommon, they can occur. So keep an eye out for tummy upsets, skin rashes, swelling of the lips and face, runny and blocked noses, sneezing, itchy watery eyes, nausea, vomiting and diarrhoea.

Please feel free to consult with your doctor or health visitor before introducing new spices into your little one's diet.

Super Spices Safe to Use in Baby Food		
Basil	Garlic powder	Pepper (black & white)
Cardamom	Ginger (ground)	Rosemary
Cinnamon	Mint	Saffron
Cloves	Nutmeg	Sage
Coriander	Oregano	Thyme
Cumin	Paprika	Turmeric
Dill	Parsley	Vanilla

How Should I Introduce Super Spices to Baby?

Introduce one spice a day into your little one's diet after first tastes and flavours have been accepted, and gradually build from there. To help, I've outlined a few easy recipes in the form of a weekly meal plan to help you transition your little one from simple fruit and vegetable tastes, over to fruit and vegetable tastes combined with aromatic flavours. Follow this daily meal plan for one week before you dive into my stage 2 recipes.

Monday – Banana and Cinnamon

Peel a ripe banana and place half in a bowl along with a small pinch of ground cinnamon. Mix and mash together well with a fork to achieve a soft, lumpy consistency. Add your baby's usual milk or cooled, boiled water to thin out the mash if necessary and serve. Alternatively, purée using a handheld blender or food processor if you are still offering your little one purées.

Tuesday – Apple and Cardamom

Wash, peel and core 2 sweet apples. Cut into chunks and place in a pan along with 4–5 tablespoons of water and a small pinch of ground cardamom. Stir and simmer, covered, on low heat for 4–5 minutes until the apple is tender. Purée or mash as necessary.

Wednesday – Plum and Vanilla

Wash and cut 2 ripe plums in half and twist to pull apart. Peel the skin using a sharp knife and remove the stones. Roughly chop the flesh, leaving them in big chunks and add to a pan. Next cut the top off a fresh vanilla pod, slice in half lengthways, to half the length of the pod and scrape out the vanilla seeds with the tip of the knife. Pop the vanilla seeds into the pan along with 2 tablespoons of water, stir and simmer, covered, on low heat until the plums

are tender (4–6 minutes). If the plums are already fairly ripe, simmer for a couple of minutes to infuse the vanilla with the flesh. Purée or mash as necessary. If the plums are too tart, add a little banana when serving. Alternatively, simmer the plums in pure apple juice.

Thursday – Butternut Squash and Cumin Purée

Place 250g (half) a butternut squash (peeled, deseeded, cubed) into a pan with 4–5 tablespoons of water and a pinch of ground cumin and stir. Simmer, covered, on low heat until tender. Mash or purée in a food processor or using a handheld blender as necessary.

Friday – Cauliflower and Turmeric Purée

Place quarter of a cauliflower (thoroughly washed, cut into small florets) in a pan with 4–5 tablespoons of water and add a pinch of ground turmeric and stir. Simmer, covered, on low heat for 8–10 minutes until tender. Purée or mash as required.

Saturday – Carrot and Coriander Purée

Peel and trim the ends off 2 medium carrots. Roughly chop the carrots and place in a pan with 2–3 tablespoons of water and a small pinch of ground coriander and stir. Simmer, covered, on low heat until tender. Pop in a food processor and blend or mash as necessary. Achieve soft lumps in a food processor by using a pulse motion.

Sunday – Peach and Ginger Purée

Wash and skin 2 ripe peaches using the same method for plums (see Wednesday). Roughly chop the flesh, leaving it in big chunks and add to a pan. Next add a pinch of ground ginger and 2 tablespoons of water and stir. Simmer, covered, on low heat until the peaches are tender (4–6 minutes). If the peaches are already fairly ripe, simmer for just a couple of minutes to infuse the ginger with the flesh. Purée the peaches in a food processor or using a handheld blender.

Super Foods & Food Groups

So we've discovered Super Spices are a fantastic edition to your little one's meals for enhancing taste and for her general health. However, we must not forget to look at major food groups Super Spices should be consumed with in order to gain optimal health benefits at mealtimes.

All foods contain some nutritional value which will be beneficial to baby, however, there are other foods naturally chock-full with an even HIGHER amount of nutrients. These foods have been labelled 'Super Foods', as they are known to have extra health benefits. As with Super Spices, they contain antioxidants, however, these antioxidants have been scientifically proven to benefit health, making them hugely important for baby's well-being and for fighting off diseases. So Super Foods are the healthy start all babies need and can be found within every food group.

Infants' Estimated Average Requirements (EAR) for Energy:

7 to 12 months: boys 717*kcal per day
girls 656*kcal per day

* Based on mixed-feeding or unknown. Slightly more calories are required for formula-fed babies. Slightly less for breast-fed babies.

(Source: UK Department of Health, SACN Dietary Reference Values for Energy)

Food Groups – Getting the Balance Right for Baby

From 7 months, your little one's diet should begin shifting towards three balanced meals a day. As she grows and requires more energy, this should gradually increase to three balanced meals and two healthy snacks per day.

There are four major food groups outlined below that baby must consume from to attain her recommended calorie intake, and to achieve a balanced diet. A balanced diet ensures your little one gets all of the vitamins and minerals she needs to grow into a healthy adult.

Food Groups	Baby's Serving Amount (per day)
Carb-rich (Starches)	3–4 servings
Fruits and Vegetables	3–4 servings
Milk and Dairy Foods	3 servings
Protein-rich	1–2 servings

In addition to 500–600ml (18fl oz–1 pint) of breastmilk or formula per day.

Carb-rich (Starches)

Being one of the largest food groups also makes it one of the most important. Bread, rice, potatoes, pasta, fortified breakfast cereals, rice, rotis (chapattis) and couscous are all included under the starchy foods umbrella and provide your baby with valuable nutrients, fibre and much-needed energy to crawl, walk and play. Potatoes are not classed as a vegetable portion due to their high starch content, so include some other vegetables in her meal as well, or serve them alongside her meal as a finger food. From 7 months onwards, feed your little one 3–4 servings of starchy foods per day, ideally with every meal.

Carb-rich Super Food: Whole Grains

Whole grains such as wholemeal bread, whole wheat pasta, brown rice and wholemeal cereals are the Super Foods of this group. They are antioxidant, anti-cancer, keep the heart healthy, and are high in fibre and in complex carbohydrates. Complex carbohydrates break down to produce glucose (a type of sugar), and when transported around the body via the blood stream, it is transformed into energy.

Although whole grain varieties are nutritionally better, feeding your little one too many high fibre foods can stop the absorption of important minerals such as iron and calcium, potentially leading to anaemia later in life and affecting mental and physical growth. Whole grains can also fill up your little one's tummy before she's eaten the necessary amount of calories required for healthy growth. With both points in mind, I opted to feed Aaliyah a combination of white and whole grain varieties of starchy foods as she grew, as they both contain complex carbohydrates.

Fruits and Vegetables

Nature has provided us with a vast array of delicious and colourful fruits and vegetables, each containing unique vitamins, minerals and fibre essential to our health. So being another large food group, take advantage of these natural sources and feed your little one a rainbow of as many different coloured fruits and vegetables as you can, to ensure you are giving her a balanced diet. Fruits and vegetables don't always need to be fresh; give them a try in dried, canned or frozen varieties.

Feed your little one fruit and vegetables in each meal, 3–4 servings per day.

Fruit and Vegetable Super Foods: The Rainbow

Red/Pink	Cherries, red grapes, guava, papaya, raspberries, red pepper, red/pink grapefruit, strawberries, tomatoes, watermelon.
Yellow/ Orange	Apricots, cantaloupe melons, carrots, lemons, mangoes, oranges, peaches, pumpkins, squash, sweet potatoes.
Green	Asparagus, avocados, broccoli, cabbage, kale, lettuce, peas, spinach, watercress.
Blue/ Purple	Aubergine, beetroots, blackberries, blueberries, black grapes, plums, prunes, raisins, raspberries.
White	Apples, bananas, cauliflower, garlic, ginger, mushrooms, onions, potatoes.

Red and Pink

Lycopene is a nutrient and part of the carotenoid family, a group of naturally occurring plant pigments and the reason for the vibrant red colour of certain fruits and vegetables.

Lycopene, one of the most powerful antioxidants, is believed to help prevent heart disease and reduce several types of cancer. The most concentrated source is found in tomatoes and must be cooked in order for the body to absorb lycopene more efficiently. Great news, as Indian cuisine involves heavy usage of tomatoes in fresh, puréed or tinned varieties, all of which are great sources of lycopene for your little one.

Lycopene, although found in small quantities, is also present in numerous Super Spices such as chilli powder, ground cinnamon, black pepper, dried parsley and dried basil.

Tomatoes are also an excellent source of vitamin C along with other red fruits and vegetables – strawberries, raspberries, papaya, red peppers and watermelon. Vitamin C is necessary for general well-being, helping to build a strong immune system, keep red blood cells healthy and support the healing of cuts and grazes. In addition, vitamin C helps the body absorb iron from food, extremely important for babies following a vegetarian diet.

Other sources of vitamin C include citrus fruits, green peppers, broccoli, Brussels sprouts, spinach, cabbage, cauliflower and white potatoes.

Yellow and Orange

Beta-carotene, one of the most common carotenoids, is responsible for the orange and yellow pigment found in particular fruits and vegetables. Beta-carotene is important for babies for its antioxidant and anti-cancer properties. It also has fabulous anti-ageing properties for us mums! When consumed, it is converted into vitamin A, another key vitamin for babies. Vitamin A is essential for healthy vision and skin, and for boosting the immune system. Beta-carotene is also found in less 'orange' vegetables such as leafy greens – spinach, kale and lettuce. In addition, beta-carotene can be found in Super Spices like dried basil, dried parsley, dried oregano, ground sage and paprika.

Citrus fruits are an excellent concentrated source of vitamin C. Vitamin C is an antioxidant and although it doesn't cure the common cold, prevents further complications such as pneumonia.

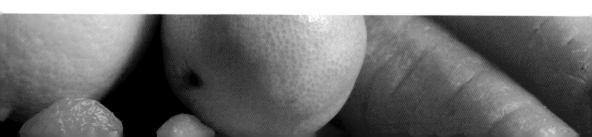

Green

Although coloured by the plant pigment chlorophyll, it's the carotenoids, lutein and zeaxanthin, found in the green group that are beneficial to health. Lutein and zeaxanthin are antioxidant and generally found in dark, leafy green vegetables – spinach and kale. They can also be found in less 'green' foods such as egg yolks, corn and in different varieties of squash. A diet rich in lutein and zeaxanthin can keep eyes healthy, leading
to a reduced risk of cataracts or age-related eye diseases later in life.

Green vegetables, and other vegetables from the cruciferous family such as broccoli, Brussels sprouts, kale, cabbage and cauliflower, are linked to research suggesting they are anti-cancer and high in vitamins A and C and B vitamins such as folate (folic acid).

B vitamins are necessary for converting food into energy, which your little one will need for crawling, walking and playing. Folic acid can be found in broccoli and Brussels sprouts, and works with vitamin B12 in the production of healthy red blood cells and nerve function. Vitamin B12 can be found in eggs, dairy foods, fish and meat.

Blue and Purple

Coloured by the plant pigment anthocyanin, found in blueberries, plums and prunes, aubergines, black grapes, raisins and black raspberries, to name just a few, research proves this carotenoid is a powerful antioxidant, helping to prevent certain types of cancer. It similarly plays a role in preventing strokes as well as diseases such as diabetes, dementia and heart disease.

Plums and prunes are extremely nutritious for babies, as they are rich in vitamins A and C, making them useful in aiding iron absorption. Also, being fibre-rich keeps little bowels healthy.

This group also contains antioxidants ellagic acid and flavonoids. Flavonoids are nutrients mainly found in dark grapes, blueberries and red berries, although they are also present in garlic and onions. Both flavonoids and ellagic acid are believed to have anti-cancer properties. Super Spices containing flavonoids include dried rosemary, black pepper and dried oregano.

White

Garlic, root ginger, white potatoes, apples, bananas, cauliflowers and onions are just a few members of the white group to provide exceptional health benefits. Garlic contains vitamin C and includes the compound

allicin, the main reason for its many health-promoting properties such as preventing heart disease and reducing cholesterol and blood pressure. Garlic also possesses antibiotic and anti-viral properties, helping to protect against cold and flu viruses.

Root ginger, another potent herb from the white group, is also used frequently in Indian cookery. It is great for aiding digestion, treating fever from coughs and colds and treating arthritis. White potatoes contain vitamin C and, in addition to being an energy-boosting starchy food, are an excellent source of potassium. Potassium is vital for heart function and is essential for the entire body, ensuring all cells, tissues and internal organs are kept in excellent working order.

Another major source of potassium from the white group is bananas. Bananas are excellent on-the-go foods for babies: no need for washing, protected in their own little yellow jackets, they are creamy, delicious and nutritious. They are fibre-rich, and contain vitamin C and vitamin B6.

Onions are heavily used in Indian home cooking and form the base of most curry sauces. This is excellent for babies as onions are high in vitamin C, anti-cancer and anti-inflammatory, helping to protect the body against infections and allergies.

So we've reached the end of the rainbow and you can see there are unquestionable benefits to eating a range of different coloured fruits and vegetables; all providing your little one with unique vitamins and minerals essential for a well-balanced diet.

Milk and Dairy Foods

Going back to our main food groups, this group includes all full-fat dairy produce – whole milk, cheese, yogurt, fromage frais and custard – all great sources of vitamin A, protein and calcium, and key to building strong teeth and bones. With the exception of whole milk, all are safe to introduce into your little one's diet from 6 months.

Whole milk MUST NOT be introduced into baby's diet as a main drink prior to the age of one, as it lacks the right balance of nutrients, vitamins and minerals. Continue with 500–600ml (18fl oz–1 pint) of either breast milk or formula until your little one's first birthday. Whole milk can, however, be used in cooking prior to the age of one.

Feed your little one three servings per day of her usual milk, to ensure she has the correct amount of calcium required for healthy growth.

Milk and Dairy Super Foods: Yogurt

Yogurt was awarded its Super Food status due to its probiotic properties which provide healthy bacteria for the gut. Gut health and good digestion are both linked to the overall health of the immune system. So it is imperative both are kept in good working order to give your little one the opportunity to fight off viruses and infections naturally.

Furthermore, yogurt is high in iodine, necessary for healthy thyroid gland function. The thyroid gland supplies hormones to the body to control growth and metabolism, vital for weight control. It is also rich in calcium and protein and is easily digestible.

Protein-rich

This group includes lean red meat, poultry, fish, eggs, nuts and pulses (e.g. beans, lentils and peas), and foods made from pulses (e.g. tofu, hummus and soya foods).

Protein is essential for healthy growth since it lives in every cell and tissue in our body. Proteins are composed of different combinations of amino acids broken down into 'essential' and 'non-essential' amino acids. Essential amino acids must be consumed through food as our bodies cannot produce them naturally. The other non-essential amino acids can be produced daily by our bodies. So protein-rich foods provide fundamental sources of essential amino acids required by adults and children to sustain and repair muscles, blood vessels, bones and internal organs.

The protein-rich group is also a wonderful source of iron, necessary for producing red blood cells to carry oxygen around the body. Good sources of iron include lean cuts of beef and lamb, dark chicken meat (legs and thighs), lentils, chickpeas, nuts and kidney beans. A lack of iron can lead to anaemia later in life.

In addition, protein-rich foods are excellent sources of B vitamins and many contain zinc. Zinc, a mineral required for processing proteins, fat and carbs, is necessary for good sense of taste and smell and for healing cuts and wounds efficiently. Exactly what your little one will need when she starts running around causing mischief!

Feed your baby one or two servings from this group every day.

Protein-rich Super Food: Oily Fish

Oily fish are Super Foods due to their high-quality protein content, plus they are rich in vitamin D and contain essential omega 3 fatty acids. Omega 3 fatty acids must be consumed through food such as salmon, mackerel and sardines, and are required for good brain function, growth and development and for keeping the heart healthy. They are also believed to be anti-inflammatory and anti-cancer.

Fats, Salt, Sugar and Oils

A fifth group exists that babies should not be exposed to, comprising sugary foods or foods high in saturated fats. Fats are essential for providing concentrated energy in children under the age of two, provided they are unsaturated fats (good fats), such as whole milk, yogurt, cheese, oily fish and lean cuts of meat. Saturated fats (bad fats) such as burgers, fried chips and sugary cakes and biscuits should be avoided.

Salt should be avoided as it can damage a baby's kidneys due to their immature digestive system. Babies under a year old need less than 1g of salt per day, which they usually get from breast milk or formula.

Age	Maximum Salt Intake
1–3 years	2g per day
4–6 years	3g per day
7–10 years	5g per day
11 years – adults	6g per day

Equally, sugar must be avoided as it can damage a baby's growing teeth. Sometimes before their teeth have even emerged! It also gives babies excess energy, leading to a higher risk of growing into overweight or obese children, which can lead to health problems later in life. Babies get their sugar from natural sources such as fruits, vegetables and their usual milk.

Oils are safe to use when cooking your little one's meals although they should be used sparingly. A good choice is to cook with oils containing polyunsaturated or monounsaturated fats such as olive, soya or rapeseed oil (i.e. pure vegetable oil). Research has shown that polyunsaturated and monounsaturated fats (good fats) are good for the heart. Alternatively, you can cook with ghee (clarified butter) commonly used in Indian cookery.

From the age of one, your baby's diet should consist of three balanced meals and two healthy snacks per day to achieve her required calorie intake. Depending on appetite, this could be three snacks per day.

When your little one reaches the budding age of two, she will still need to consume three meals and 2–3 snacks per day, although her serving requirement from each food group will change. Up to the age of five, her diet will gradually shift towards that of an adult. So from two, the UK 'eatwell plate' (page 28) can be applied to her diet.

Food Groups – Getting the Balance Right for Toddler

Toddlers Estimated Average Requirements (EAR) for Energy:

1 year	Boys 764 kcal per day
	Girls 716 kcal per day
2 years	Boys 1003 kcal per day
	Girls 931 kcal per day
3 years	Boys 1170 kcal per day
	Girls 1075 kcal per day

(Source: UK Department of Health, SACN Dietary Reference Values for Energy)

The eatwell plate is a handy visual guide to assist you in understanding how much of what your little one eats should come from each food group, including all of her snack requirements. An extensively tested model by the UK Department of Health, it represents how different foods contribute towards the overall balance of a healthy diet for an adult or child, and is an excellent tool you can refer to for the whole family.

Depending on appetite and what mood your little one is in, she may binge on food one day and barely eat anything the next. So use the eatwell plate as a guide to achieve a healthy balanced diet over a period of time (a week rather than a day), and continue offering nutrient-rich foods, new tastes and textures where you can to keep food interesting.

The eatwell plate

Use the eatwell plate to help you get the balance right.
It shows how much of what you eat should come from each food group.

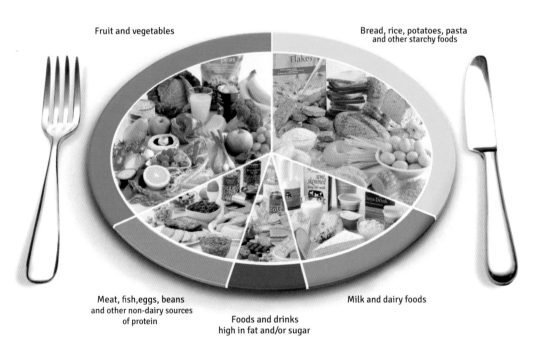

Fruit and vegetables

Bread, rice, potatoes, pasta and other starchy foods

Meat, fish, eggs, beans and other non-dairy sources of protein

Foods and drinks high in fat and/or sugar

Milk and dairy foods

Welsh Government in association with Department of Health, the Scottish Government and the Food Standards Agency in Northern Ireland

5 a-day! Carb-rich (Starches) – Bread, Rice, Potatoes, Pasta and other Starchy Foods

Eat plenty. At least one third of your little one's food intake should be starchy foods. So from the age of two, gradually increase your little one's servings from three or four starchy foods per day to five a day. Continue feeding her a combination of white and wholemeal varieties, to ensure she gets the correct amount of calories required for healthy growth and slow release energy.

5 a-day! Fruits and Vegetables

Fruits and vegetables make up another third of your little one's food requirements. So eat plenty and, as with starchy foods, increase your baby's servings gradually from three or four per day to at least five servings per day. One serving equates to the amount your little one can hold in her hand.

As your baby grows, continue feeding her a rainbow of as many different coloured fruits and vegetables in each meal as you can, to maintain her balanced diet. This can be within meals or served separately as a finger food.

3 a-day! Milk and Dairy Foods

Milk is no longer the main source of nutrients for your little one, but she will need to consume some combined with other dairy foods. While your baby's serving amount hasn't changed, she will still need three servings of calcium per day. You can reduce the amount of milk you are offering (from the 500–600ml/18fl oz–1 pint per day) and increase the amount of other dairy foods in your baby's diet instead.

Your baby's 3 a-day serving can be achieved through 300ml (½ pint) of milk offered throughout the day as a drink with meals.

Or by serving one 100ml (3½fl oz) beaker of milk as a drink, and later offering some other dairy foods, such as cheese, yogurt, fromage frais or rice pudding. Also, from the age of two, provided she is not underweight and is growing well, you can move your little one on to semi-skimmed milk if you wish.

The best alternative drink to milk is tap water. Serve 100ml (3½fl oz) tap water 6–8 times throughout the day with meals and snacks, ideally in a free-flow beaker.

As your little one approaches five, choose lower fat alternatives where possible to avoid unnecessary weight gain, or offer higher fat versions infrequently or in smaller amounts.

2 a-day! Protein-rich – Meat, Fish, Eggs, Beans and other Non-dairy Sources of Protein

If you aren't already offering your baby two servings of protein-rich foods per day, it's a good time to start. This can be achieved through serving scrambled eggs, tinned fish (such as tuna and salmon), small fillets of fish (such as haddock, cod or salmon), peanut butter, lentils, beef or chicken.

Fish should be served at least twice a week and one of these servings should be oily fish, such as salmon, sardines or mackerel.

Continue to cook with lean servings of meat where possible as these contain lower amounts of fat. Alternatively, eat higher fat versions infrequently or in smaller amounts.

If you are feeding your little one a vegetarian diet, she will need at least 3 servings of protein-rich foods per day.

Foods and Drinks High in Fat and/or Sugar

Ideally your little one should not be eating anything from this food group. In practice, however, I'm fully aware this isn't always possible! By this stage, your little one will no doubt have been introduced to a few sweet treats either by yourself or by members of the family. So offer just a small amount and try to keep these to a minimum, only after a main meal to avoid tooth decay and unnecessary weight gain. Alternatively, offer my Sweet Super Meals (page 99) as a healthy means to satisfy your little one's sweet tooth. Likewise, salt should be kept to a minimum (see guidelines on page 27).

Foods to Avoid and Potential Allergens	Reason	Safe to Introduce at:
Cow's Milk (drink)	Lacks the right balance of nutrients, vitamins and minerals in infants under one. It is suitable for cooking.	1 year + As a main drink.
Fizzy Drinks, Squash, Fruit Juices	Contain added sugar which can lead to tooth decay and weight gain. Fruit juices can be diluted one part juice to 10 parts water.	Not required. Offer sips of water with meals. Diluted fruit juices can be offered occasionally.
Hard/Small Round Foods – apple chunks, raw carrot sticks, grapes, blueberries	Choking hazard.	6 months + Lightly steam hard foods to soften them. Or cut round, softer fruits into small pieces.
Honey	Occasionally contains bacteria causing Infant botulism (serious illness of the intestines). Also a sugar so can cause tooth decay.	1 year +
Low-fat Foods – milk, yogurt, cheese	Fat is an important source of concentrated energy for babies and toddlers, so full-fat varieties are essential for a minimum of 2 years.	2 years +
Raw Eggs	Undercooked eggs may cause food poisoning. Eggs are also an allergen in some infants.	6 months + Whole egg (yolk and white) should be cooked thoroughly.
Raw Shellfish	Can cause food poisoning.	Not required.
Salt	Can damage a baby's kidneys.	1 year + Limited amounts only.
Shark, Swordfish, Marlin.	Contain high levels of mercury which can affect a baby's developing nervous system.	Not required. Offer oily fish instead i.e. tuna, salmon, mackerel.
Sweet Foods – Indian sweets (mithai), chocolate, sweets.	Contain added sugar and saturated fat.	Not required.
Tea and Coffee (drink)	Reduces iron absorption and caffeine disrupts baby's sleep.	Not required. Offer sips of water with meals.
Whole nuts – peanuts included	Choking hazard. However, can be crushed, ground or given to babies in the form of peanut butter after 6 months provided baby is not allergic.	5 years +

Getting Started — The Essentials

To get started you'll need to invest in some essentials for the kitchen. The most important being... spices! Spices can be very confusing if you haven't used them before, all with their own unique colours, flavours and aromas. Where do you start? Well, to take the confusion away, I have compiled two essential **'Spice Starter Kits'**.

'Spice Starter Kit 1' includes all of the core aromatic spices I use in my Stage 2 recipes. 'Spice Starter Kit 2' includes additional aromatic spices you will need to use alongside 'Spice Starter Kit 1', for Stages 3 and 4 recipes. I would recommend investing in 'Spice Starter Kit 1' first, and as your little one progresses into toddlerhood, then investing in 'Spice Starter Kit 2'.

Additional aromatic spices are used within Stages 2, 3 and 4 recipes such as saffron, nutmeg, mint and oregano amongst others. However, these spices are used infrequently so they can be bought when necessary.

Spice Advice

Spices are available in whole and ground varieties. If you prefer, you can buy spices whole and use a pestle and mortar to grind them into a powder. For convenience, however, I keep both whole and ground spices in the cupboard.

IMPORTANT: ensure all spices you buy are produced by reputable brands and sealed with a clear expiry date on the packet. If you are unfamiliar with spice brands, I would recommend buying them from well-known supermarkets only. Once the packet is opened, store in a clean, dry, airtight container away from sunlight, to ensure the spices remain fresh for your baby.

Spice Starter Kit 1 (Stage 2)
Black pepper (ground)
Cardamom pods (green – ground or whole)
Cinnamon (ground)
Coriander (ground)
Cumin (ground)
Garlic (fresh or ready minced)
Ginger (fresh or ready minced)
Turmeric (ground)

Spice Starter Kit 2 (Stages 3 & 4)
Black peppercorns (whole)
Cardamom pods (black, whole)
Cinnamon sticks (whole)
Cloves (whole)
Cumin seeds (whole)
Garam masala (ground)
Mild paprika (ground)

Other Essential Equipment and Ingredients:

* Baby/toddler weaning bowls
* 50 tb-tipped weaning spoons
* Bibs and/or long-sleeved bibs
* Food processer/handheld blender
* High-chair (with tray)
* Large-based non-stick frying pan
* Masher
* Medium and large pots/pans (with lids)
* Olive oil
* Onions
* Pestle and mortar (optional)
* Steamer (optional)
* Unsalted butter
* Wooden spoon

Worth Knowing

* Vitamins A, C and D are key vitamins babies will need for healthy growth. The UK Department of Health recommends supplements should be given to children from six months to five years old who aren't following a varied diet. Please check with your health visitor or doctor for more details.

* If your weekly shopping budget allows, buy organic produce for your baby as it's free from artificial fertilisers and ensures a GM (genetically modified)-free diet. Almost everything nowadays has an organic counterpart; milk, meat, vegetables, butter, cheese and yogurt. All are readily available from supermarkets.

* If you are heating your little one's food in the microwave, stir the food thoroughly to ensure there are no hot spots. You must ALWAYS test the temperature of your baby's food before serving.

* Curries taste their finest when you let them stand for about 30 minutes to an hour before serving, giving the spices a chance to soak into the meat, fish or vegetables. Even if the curries are refrigerated or frozen, the longer they stand, the better they taste!

* If you want to feed your little one curry with roti and she insists on feeding herself, break the roti into small pieces, top with curry and mix it altogether. She will happily eat the curry soaked pieces of roti (and any meat or vegetables) with her fingers, transforming the curry into a handy finger food.

Right then, we've gone through everything you'll need to know in order to cook your own Super Meals, so let's get cooking!

Veggie Super Meals

The Stage 2 recipes in this chapter are the scrumptious vegetarian Super Meals I fed Aaliyah when she moved on from Stage 1 puréed fruits and veggies. I mashed the vegetables within these meals to achieve those much-needed soft lumps to help her learn to chew.

Chewing, an essential motor skill for baby, gives the jaw, lips and tongue muscles an excellent workout. A crucial skill to master, because the muscles used for chewing are the same muscles required to help baby develop speech later in childhood.

Don't worry if your baby is still a 'gummy baby' (doesn't have any teeth) at this stage, her hard little gums will be able to power through soft lumps easily enough.

You can offer meat and poultry to babies from 7 months of age in cooked, puréed form only, as meat proteins are not as easy to digest as vegetables. For this reason, I chose to wait until Aaliyah's digestive system had matured before introducing meat into her diet. In the meantime, I fed Aaliyah fish, eggs and lentils to ensure there were no protein shortfalls in her diet.

Milk feeds are still a huge part of baby's diet. She will need 500–600ml (18fl oz–1 pint) per day to ensure she receives the necessary amount of calcium required for healthy growth. So continue feeding your little one either breast milk or formula.

Sweet Potato, Apple and Dhal Curry

Dhal (lentils) are a staple in many Indian and Pakistani households and are highly recommended for those following a strict vegetarian diet. The lentils provide a valuable source of protein that babies need for healthy growth, ensuring vegetarian babies do not miss important nutrients from the protein-rich food group.

1 tbsp olive oil
1 small onion – peeled, finely chopped
¼ tsp minced ginger
¼ tsp minced garlic
Pinch of ground cumin
¼ tsp ground cinnamon
125g (4oz) red lentils – soaked in water (10 mins), washed, drained
1 small sweet potato – washed, peeled, cubed
600ml (1 pint) water
1 sweet apple – peeled, cored, chopped into small chunks

Heat the oil in a pot, add the onion and stir-fry for 3–4 mins. Turn to low heat and add the ginger, garlic, cumin and cinnamon and stir-fry for a further 30 secs.

Add the lentils to the pot, along with the sweet potato, cover with the water and stir. Bring to the boil and simmer (uncovered) on medium heat for 20 mins, until both the lentils and potato are tender.

While the lentils and potato are cooking, steam the apple chunks using a steamer, or in the microwave by placing them in a microwavable dish and adding 2 tablespoons of water. Cover the dish with either a lid (leaving a small vent) or cling film (piercing a few holes), and steam on high for 1½–2 mins until tender.

Once cooked, drain the excess water and add to the curry at the end. Stir and mash the whole curry to a consistency your little one will be comfortable eating. Delicious served on its own or with rice or roti for toddlers.

Ratatouille

Inspired by the French classic, this Super Meal is chock-full of a range of vitamins, minerals and antioxidant and anti-cancer properties from a combination of the red, purple, green and white vegetables within this meal. Tomatoes, onions and courgettes are all excellent sources of vitamin C, contributing towards a healthy immune system. Courgettes are also rich in potassium, wonderful for heart health and for helping the body to absorb calcium for strong teeth and bones.

1 tbsp olive oil
1 onion – peeled, chopped
½ tsp minced garlic
2 baby aubergines – washed, peeled, finely diced
1 small courgette – washed, finely diced
½ red pepper – washed, deseeded, finely diced
1 x 200g (7oz) tin chopped tomatoes
¼ tsp dried oregano
Pinch of ground black pepper
75ml (3fl oz) water
30g (1¼oz) medium Cheddar cheese – grated (optional)

Heat the oil in a large frying pan, add the onion and stir-fry on medium-low heat for 2–3 mins. Add the garlic, aubergines, courgette, red pepper and stir-fry for 10 mins.

Add the tomatoes, oregano, black pepper and water and stir. Simmer (covered) on medium–low heat for another 10 mins. Check halfway through, if the sauce looks dry add some water, replace the lid and continue to cook.

When all of the vegetables are tender, turn off the heat, sprinkle over the cheese (if using) and fold in until melted. Blend if necessary to achieve the required lumpy consistency using a pulse motion. Serve on its own or with cooked pasta.

Kitchri

'Kitchri', yellow lentil rice, is traditionally eaten with 'Kadhi', yogurt soup. I however, chose to serve it alongside most curries I fed Aaliyah because kitchri is 'Super Rice' in my opinion. Here's why: the rice provides complex carbohydrates for energy, the lentils add protein, turmeric adds a powerful cold- and flu-preventing ingredient, and cardamom acts as a natural painkiller for teething. I rest my case!

1 tbsp yellow lentils (toor dhal)
 – soaked in water (10 mins),
 washed, drained
100g (3½oz) brown basmati
 rice – soaked in water
 (10 mins), washed, drained
Pinch of ground turmeric
Pinch of ground cardamom –
 green
1 tbsp vegetable oil
600ml (1 pint) water

Add the lentils, rice, turmeric, cardamom, oil and water to a pot and stir.

Bring to the boil and simmer (covered) on low heat for 40–45 mins, until the lentils and rice are both tender and all of the water has been absorbed. The rice should be overcooked to a mushy consistency, which will make it easier for baby to chew and swallow.

Serve warm as an accompaniment to curry or as a yummy snack by adding my Bananaberry Raita (page 101) to the kitchri.

Mint and Coriander Veggie Stew

Hearty and delicious! Not only is this a well-balanced meal utilising almost every food group, the antioxidant spice mint adds extra health benefits by aiding digestion and protecting against unsettled tummies. Mint is also great for opening congested nasal and throat passages, so I would recommend this comforting Super Meal if your little one has a cold or the flu.

1 tbsp olive oil
1 onion – peeled, chopped
¼ tsp minced ginger
¼ tsp minced garlic
Pinch of ground coriander
Pinch of ground turmeric
1 tbsp red lentils – soaked
   in water (10 mins), washed,
   drained
1 tbsp yellow lentils (toor dhal)
   – soaked in water (10 mins),
   washed, drained
1 small white potato –
   washed, peeled, cubed
1 medium carrot – washed,
   peeled, finely chopped
80g (3oz) cherry tomatoes –
   washed, deseeded, chopped
600ml (1 pint) water
1 bay leaf
Pinch of dried mint

Heat the oil in a pot, add the onion and stir-fry for 3–4 mins. Turn to low heat and add the ginger, garlic, coriander and turmeric. Continue to stir-fry for 30 secs–1 min until the aroma from the spices has been released.

Add the red and yellow lentils to the pot along with the potato, carrot and tomatoes and stir to coat the vegetables in the delicious spices. Pour the water into the pot and add the bay leaf and mint. Bring to the boil and simmer (covered) on low heat until tender.

Once tender, gently break the vegetables into soft lumps using the back of your wooden spoon. Remove the bay leaf and serve warm. Delicious served on its own or, for a heavier meal, serve with buttered soft bread.

Mixed Veggies in Coconut Milk

UK healthcare professionals actively campaign 'breast is best' for newborn babies due to the perfect nutritional content of breast milk, and its immune-boosting compound 'lauric acid'. Another source of lauric acid, however, can be found in coconut milk. So feeding your little one this creamy scrummy curry should help to keep cold and flu viruses at bay.

1 tbsp olive oil
1 small onion – peeled, chopped
½ tsp minced garlic
¼ tsp minced ginger
Pinch of ground turmeric
Pinch of ground cumin
Pinch of ground coriander
1 medium parsnip – washed, peeled, chopped
80g (3oz) green beans – washed, ends chopped off, halved
200g (7oz) cauliflower florets – washed, chopped (no stems)
100g (3½oz) tinned sweetcorn (no added salt) – drained
250ml (8fl oz) unsweetened coconut milk

Heat the oil in a pot, add the onion and stir-fry on medium-low heat for 3–4 mins until soft and golden. Turn to low heat and add the garlic, ginger, turmeric, cumin and coriander and stir-fry for a further 30 secs–1 min.

Add all of the remaining vegetables to the pot along with the coconut milk and stir. Bring to the boil and simmer (covered) on a medium-low heat for 6–8 mins until all of the vegetables are tender.

Once cooked, mash the vegetables to a soft lumpy consistency using either a masher or food processor using a pulse motion.

Serve to baby warm or, for toddlers, serve with rice or roti for a heavier meal.

Veggie Korma

I love this korma! It's simple, nutritious and is another yummy recipe with the subtle naturally sweet taste of the exotic coconut. Not widely accepted as a Super Food due to its fat content, coconuts are extremely nutritious. Fibre-rich and a good source of vitamins C and E, B vitamins, iron and calcium. With all of these health benefits and more, coconuts are definitely Super Foods in my opinion.

1 tbsp olive oil
1 tomato – washed,
    deseeded, grated
Pinch of ground turmeric
Pinch of ground cumin
¼ tsp minced garlic
1 medium white potato –
    washed, peeled, cubed
2 tbsp unsweetened
    desiccated coconut
200ml (7fl oz) water
1 medium carrot – washed,
    peeled, chopped
40g (1½oz) peas –
    frozen, washed

Heat the oil in a pot and add the tomato, turmeric, cumin and garlic and stir-fry for 1–2 mins. Add the potato, coconut and water. Stir and bring to the boil. Simmer (covered) on low heat for 15–20 mins until tender. Mash and set aside.

While the potato mixture is simmering, steam the carrot and peas in either a steamer, or in the microwave by placing them in a microwavable dish and adding 2 tablespoons of water. Cover the dish with either a lid (leaving a small vent) or cling film (piercing a few holes), and steam on high for 1–1½ mins. Drain and add to the mashed potato mixture.

Further mash or blend as necessary using a pulse motion. Serve to baby warm.

Rainbow Veggie Pie

This scrumptious pie epitomizes the concept of 'feeding your little one a rainbow'. Packed with red, green, orange and white vegetables, this pie is loaded with a range of vitamins and minerals perfectly balanced for your little one. Also including starchy foods and dairy, this pie utilises almost every food group.

1 tbsp olive oil
1 small onion – peeled, chopped
½ tsp minced garlic
1 tomato – washed, deseeded, chopped
Pinch of ground cumin
Pinch of ground coriander
1 medium carrot – washed, peeled, chopped
1 small sweet potato – washed, peeled, cubed
1 medium white potato – washed, peeled, cubed
400ml (14fl oz) water
80g (3oz) broccoli florets – washed, chopped (no stems)
60g (2½oz) peas – frozen, washed
40g (1½oz) medium Cheddar cheese – grated
1–2 tbsp whole milk (optional)

Heat the oil in a large pot, add the onion and stir-fry on medium-low heat for 3–4 mins until soft and lightly golden. Turn to low heat and add the garlic, tomato, cumin and coriander and stir-fry for 2 mins.

Add the carrot, sweet potato and white potato, pour in the water and stir. Bring to the boil and simmer (covered) on medium-low heat for 15 mins. Add the broccoli and peas and continue to simmer for a further 5–7 mins or until all of the vegetables are tender.

Sprinkle the cheese over the cooked vegetables in the pot, fold in until melted and mash to achieve a soft lumpy consistency. Add some milk or cooled boiled water to make it smoother if necessary. Serve to baby warm.

Warming Carrot and Broccoli Soup

I created this soup when Aaliyah suffered from her first cold. It includes valuable cold- and flu-fighting ingredients. The broccoli and red pepper provide the vitamin C, the garlic's anti-viral properties provide cold and flu protection, and the ginger is excellent for treating fever and coughs. Combined with powerful Super Spices, this soup will chase that pesky cold away in no time.

1 tbsp olive oil
1 onion – peeled, chopped
1 whole cardamom pod – green
1 whole clove
½ tsp minced ginger
½ tsp minced garlic
2 medium carrots – washed, peeled, diced
200g (7oz) broccoli – washed, chopped (no stems)
1 red pepper – washed, deseeded, chopped
Pinch of ground turmeric
Pinch of ground black pepper
¼ tsp ground cumin
300ml (½ pint) water

Heat the oil in a pot and add the onion, cardamom and clove and stir-fry on medium-low heat for 2–3 mins. Then add the ginger and garlic and stir-fry on low heat for a further 30 secs–1 min.

Add the remaining vegetables to the pot followed by the turmeric, black pepper and cumin and stir. Pour the water into the pot, bring to the boil and simmer (covered) on a medium–low heat for 6–8 mins until all of the vegetables are tender.

Allow to cool and blend until smooth. Serve to baby warm on its own or with soft white bread.

IMPORTANT: remove the cardamom pod and clove before serving to baby.

Yummy Spiced Potato Pie

This Indian-influenced potato pie is lightly flavoured with lots of traditional fragrant spices which complement the white and sweet potatoes beautifully. Bursting with beta-carotene goodness this pie is great for healthy eyes and skin. The peas also provide antioxidant and anti-inflammatory properties and are high in vitamin K – necessary for healing wounds and healthy bones – making this scrummy pie wonderfully nutritious.

1 medium white potato –
  washed, peeled, cubed
1 medium sweet potato –
  washed, peeled, cubed
1 tbsp olive oil
1 onion – peeled,
  finely chopped
¼ tsp minced garlic
Pinch of ground turmeric
Pinch of ground cumin
Pinch of ground coriander
Pinch of ground black pepper
60g (2½oz) peas – frozen,
  washed
1 tsp unsalted butter
2 tbsp whole milk

Place the white and sweet potatoes in a pot and cover with cold water. Bring to the boil and simmer (uncovered) on medium-high heat for 10–12 mins until tender.

While the potatoes are boiling, heat the oil in a frying pan and add the onion. Stir-fry on medium-low heat until soft and golden. Add the garlic, turmeric, cumin, coriander and black pepper and stir-fry for 30 secs–1 min to lightly cook the spices, then set aside.

Next steam the peas in a steamer, or in the microwave by placing them in a microwavable dish and adding 2 tablespoons of water. Cover the dish with either a lid (leaving a small vent) or cling film (piercing a few holes), and steam on high for 1–1½ mins. Drain and set aside.

Once the potatoes are cooked, drain, place in a bowl and add the peas, butter and milk and mash the potatoes until smooth. Add the spiced onion and combine for a creamy, tasty pie. If the consistency is too heavy, add some extra milk. Serve to baby warm.

Festive Roasted Vegetable Mash

A great one for the festive period, this meal is loaded with traditional Christmas flavours for baby – apples, rosemary, carrots and parsnips with a hint of Indian spices. Roasting vegetables is a fabulous way to maintain flavour and nutrients, so rest assured your little one will reap the health benefits of this meal. The vitamin A (in the form of beta-carotene) from the carrots, and the Super Spice cumin, both help to support the development of a strong and healthy immune system.

1½ tsp olive oil
¼ tsp minced garlic
Pinch of ground black pepper
Pinch of ground cumin
1 medium carrot – washed, peeled, sliced (diagonally) into 1cm (½in) pieces
1 medium parsnip – washed, peeled, sliced (diagonally) into 1cm (½in) pieces
2 small sprigs of rosemary
Pure unsweetened apple juice

Preheat the oven to 220°C/425°F/gas mark 7.

Add olive oil, garlic, black pepper and cumin to a bowl and stir. Then add the vegetables to the bowl and coat with the seasoning.

Lay the vegetables flat on top of a foil-covered baking tray and add 2 small sprigs of rosemary, on either side of the tray for a light flavour while roasting. Place the baking tray on the middle shelf of the oven and roast for 20–25 mins until tender, turning over the vegetables halfway through.

Once tender, remove from the oven and take out the rosemary sprigs. Mash or purée the mixture as necessary and use as much apple juice as required to loosen the mash. Serve to baby warm.

Alternatively, offer the roasted vegetables to your little one as a selection of finger foods when she is ready.

Butternut Squash, Apricot and Dhal Curry

My 'Super Orange' curry! Loaded with all things deliciously orange and rich in beta-carotene (vitamin A) – great for healthy eyes, skin and immune system. Perfect for toddlers, this one goes up a level in the spice and flavour stakes. A healthy yet unusual curry combination that I guarantee your little one will enjoy.

2 tbsp olive oil
1 onion – peeled, chopped
1 tsp minced garlic
1 tsp minced ginger
1 x 200g (7oz) tin chopped tomatoes
½ tsp ground garam masala
¼ tsp ground cumin
¼ tsp ground coriander
100g (3½oz) red lentils – soaked in water (10 mins), washed, drained
½ butternut squash – peeled, deseeded, cut into 2.5cm (1in) chunks
60g (2½oz) dried apricots – finely chopped
1 tbsp unsweetened desiccated coconut
600ml (1 pint) water

Heat the oil in a pot, add the onion and stir-fry on medium-low heat for 5 mins until golden brown. Add the garlic and ginger and stir-fry for 30 secs–1 min, then add the tomatoes, garam masala, cumin and coriander and stir-fry for a further 2 mins to lightly cook the spices.

Finally, add the lentils, squash, apricots, coconut and water and stir. Bring to the boil and simmer (covered) on medium-low heat for 20–25 mins until the lentils are cooked and the squash is tender and breaks apart easily.

Serve with quinoa, roti or mushed rice.

Indian Vegetable Paella

A delicious, fragrant paella packed with tender chunky vegetables, a firm favourite with Aaliyah. The bright sun-yellow rice acquires its colour from turmeric, used as a natural colouring agent for generations. Turmeric, in addition to being a cold- and flu- prevention remedy, is a source of iron and manganese. Iron is vital for transporting oxygen around the body, and the antioxidant mineral manganese is necessary for healthy brain and nerve function.

100g (3½oz) white basmati
   rice – washed, drained
350ml (12fl oz) hot vegetable
   stock – baby-friendly
¼ tsp ground turmeric
1½ tsp vegetable oil
3 saffron strands
1½ tsp olive oil
50g (2oz) red pepper –
   washed, deseeded,
   finely diced
50g (2oz) courgette –
   washed, finely diced
1 tsp minced garlic
Pinch of ground black pepper
¼ tsp dried mixed herbs

Place the rice in a pot, pour over the stock, add the turmeric, vegetable oil and saffron and stir. Bring to the boil and simmer (covered) on low heat for 10 mins or until tender.

While the rice is cooking, heat the olive oil in a frying pan and toss in the red pepper, courgette, garlic, black pepper and dried mixed herbs. Stir-fry for 6–7 mins until tender.

Once the rice is cooked, add to the frying pan and combine with the vegetables. Mash or blend if necessary and serve to baby warm.

Quick Cumin Spaghetti

Being so quick and simple to cook, I prepare this meal fresh every time. Cooked using whole cumin seeds, these Super Spices are tiny yet offer a unique peppery taste which adds lots of flavour to this meal. Equally, they are iron-rich, excellent for digestion and great for boosting baby's immune system to help keep all of those horrible viruses at bay.

20g (¾oz) spaghetti –
    broken into small pieces
40g (1½oz) broccoli florets
    washed, chopped (no stems)
40g (1½oz) carrots –
    washed, peeled, diced
1 tbsp olive oil
¼ tsp cumin seeds
½ tsp minced garlic
Pinch of ground black pepper
¼ tsp dried mixed herbs

Cook the spaghetti pieces according to the packet instructions.

Meanwhile, steam the broccoli and carrots in a steamer, or in the microwave by placing them in a microwavable dish and adding 2 tablespoons of water. Cover the dish with either a lid (leaving a small vent) or cling film (piercing a few holes), and steam on high for 1–1½ mins until tender. Once cooked, drain off the excess water and set aside.

Heat the oil in a frying pan on low heat and add the cumin seeds, garlic, black pepper and herbs. Stir-fry for 2–3 mins to lightly cook the spices. Then add the steamed vegetables and stir-fry altogether for another min.

Drain the cooked spaghetti, toss into the frying pan with the vegetables and combine well. Serve to baby warm.

Quinoa Pilaf with Mixed Veggies

Quinoa ('keen-wa'), a tiny grain but a nutritional heavy weight, is great for babies, especially vegetarian babies. Wheat-free, anti-inflammatory, plus a source of calcium, vitamin E, B vitamins and fibre. It is also a complete protein due to its essential amino acid content so is excellent for strong growth and keeping the whole body healthy.

1½ tbsp olive oil
1 onion – peeled, chopped
½ tsp minced ginger
1 tsp minced garlic
1 tomato – washed, deseeded, diced
50g (2oz) cauliflower florets – washed, chopped (no stems)
40g (1½oz) peas – frozen, washed
1 medium carrot – washed, peeled, finely diced
Juice of ½ lemon – ensuring no seeds fall in
½ tsp ground garam masala
½ tsp ground coriander
¼ tsp ground turmeric
80g (3oz) quinoa – soaked in water (10 mins), washed, drained
300ml (½ pint) water

Heat the oil in a pot, add the onion and stir-fry on medium-low heat for 3 mins until soft. Add the ginger and garlic and stir-fry for a further 30 secs–1 min, then add the tomato, cauliflower, peas, carrot, lemon juice and spices (garam masala, coriander and turmeric). Stir everything together so the vegetables are coated in the delicious spices and stir-fry for 2 mins.

Finally, add the quinoa to the pot along with the water and stir. Bring to the boil and simmer (covered) on low heat for 20–25 mins until all of the vegetables are tender (checking halfway through). Serve to baby warm with my Mint Yogurt Raita (page 109).

Alternatively, steam the cauliflower, peas and carrot separately in either a steamer, or in the microwave by placing them in a microwavable dish and adding 2 tablespoons of water. Cover the dish with either a lid (leaving a small vent) or cling film (piercing a few holes), and steam on high for 1–2 mins or until tender. Stir into the cooked quinoa mixture and serve.

Fish Super Meals

Stage 2 | 7 Months Plus
Stage 3 | 10 Months Plus

As mentioned, fish was a vital part of Aaliyah's diet from the age of 7 months because I chose not to feed her meat until she was 10 months old, making fish a fantastic meat-protein substitute.

To begin with I introduced mild-tasting white fish into her diet – cod, coley and pollock amongst others. I then followed up with slightly stronger-tasting oily fish – salmon and tuna.

I loved just how much Aaliyah enjoyed eating fish! Rich in omega 3 fatty acids, a great source of essential amino acids (protein) and excellent for helping the body absorb iron, fish was a big winner for me. Also, due to the fact that fish is so quick and easy to cook, being a mother and having a million things to do meant fish was at the top of my list for cooking quick, wholesome meals.

I kept bags of freshly frozen white fish and salmon in the freezer. Whenever I decided today was 'fish day' or was short for time, I'd simply take one fillet out of the freezer and poach it in the microwave. It was cooked and flaky within a matter of minutes.

A little reminder:

❊ Avoid fish containing high levels of mercury (shark, swordfish and marlin), as these can affect a baby's developing nervous system.

❊ Ensure all bones have been removed before serving.

Fish Pie with Pepper and Coriander

White fish, although not containing the same Super Food health benefits as oily fish, still has wonderful health benefits for your little one. It isprotein-rich and high in B vitamins providing lots of energy. Combined with the black pepper and coriander to aid digestion, this is a perfect first fish dish for baby.

2 small white potatoes –
   peeled, washed, cubed
1 tbsp olive oil
1 onion – peeled, finely
   chopped
¼ tsp minced garlic
Pinch of ground turmeric
Pinch of ground cumin
Pinch of ground coriander
Pinch of ground black pepper
1 x 100g (3½oz) white fish
   fillet (skinless, boneless)
1 tsp unsalted butter –
   softened
4 tbsp whole milk

Place the potatoes in a pot and cover with cold water. Bring to the boil and simmer for 15 mins until tender.

While the potatoes are boiling, heat the oil in a frying pan, add the onion and stir-fry for 3–4 mins until golden. Then add the garlic and all four spices and stir-fry for a further 30 secs– 1 min, then set aside.

Place the fish in a microwavable dish, gently rub in the butter and spoon over half of the milk. Cover the dish with either a lid (leaving a small vent) or cling film (piercing a few holes), and poach in the microwave on high for 1½– 2 mins until the fish is flaky. Check halfway through to ensure the fish does not overcook.

Once the potatoes are cooked, drain and place in a bowl. Add the remaining milk (along with the buttery milk the fish was cooked in) and mash the potatoes until smooth. Add the spiced onion and flake the fish into the mash, ensuring there are no sneaky bones left. Combine together for a creamy, luscious pie. If the pie consistency is too heavy for baby, add some extra milk. Serve warm.

Sweet Fish and Fruit Curry

A creamy, super-quick fish curry with just the right amount of sweetness and spice to tickle little taste buds without overwhelming them. This curry is protein-rich and packed with fruity Super Food goodness from the apple, pear and banana. These fruits are rich in antioxidants and high in fibre, keeping little bowels healthy by preventing constipation.

1 sweet apple – peeled, cored, cubed
1 ripe pear – peeled, cored, cubed
1 banana – peeled, sliced
2 tbsp plain unsweetened yogurt
150ml (¼ pint) whole milk
¼ tsp minced ginger
¼ tsp minced garlic
¼ tsp ground cumin
¼ tsp ground coriander
Pinch of ground black pepper
Pinch of ground turmeric
1 x 100g (3½oz) white fish fillet (skinless, boneless) – cut into 2.5cm (1in) chunks

Place the fruits, yogurt, milk, ginger, garlic and spices (cumin, coriander, black pepper and turmeric) into a blender and blend until smooth. Pour the fruity mixture into a pot, bring to the boil and simmer (uncovered) on low heat for 5 mins to ensure all the spices are cooked through, stirring occasionally.

Add the fish chunks to the sauce and continue to simmer for a further 5–6 mins, until the fish is flaky and breaks apart easily. Serve with mushy rice, Kitchri (page 40) or Roti Sticks (page 88).

IMPORTANT: ensure there are no fish bones included within baby's serving. Simply break the fish pieces with your fingers to check just before serving.

Creamy Tuna Loaded Potato Skins

A fab first tuna recipe for your little one, as the deep flavour of the tuna is nicely disguised amongst the yummy sweet potato. A great way to introduce this wonderful fish into your baby's diet! Rich in omega 3 fatty acids, high-quality protein (essential amino acids), selenium and B vitamins.

1 medium sweet potato – scrubbed, washed, pricked all over
90g (3¼oz) tinned tuna (in spring water) – drained
1 tbsp full-fat cream cheese
Pinch of ground black pepper
Pinch of dried mixed herbs (optional)

Place the sweet potato in the microwave and cook on high for 6–7 mins until tender to the touch. Once cooled (but still warm enough to melt the cream cheese), cut the potato in half lengthways, scoop out the flesh and place it in a bowl. Reserve the jackets, if you wish.

Flake in the tuna and add the cream cheese, black pepper and mixed herbs. Combine and mash all of the ingredients together, while ensuring some soft lumps have been left. Spoon the mixture back into the jackets if you wish, although it is not essential. Serve to baby warm.

Desi Mac 'n' Cheese with Tuna

An Indian twist on a British school dinner classic! Packed with protein and complex carbohydrates vital for energy, this meal is extremely versatile. Exclude the tuna for a vegetarian meal, chop up cooked macaroni for spoon-feeding, or keep the macaroni pasta whole and serve as a finger food.

80g (3oz) macaroni pasta

Tomato masala:
1 tbsp olive oil
½ onion – peeled, chopped
½ tsp minced garlic
½ tsp minced ginger
1 tomato – washed,
    deseeded, chopped
¼ tsp dried oregano

White sauce:
2 tbsp unsalted butter
2 tbsp plain flour
350ml (12fl oz) whole milk
Pinch of ground nutmeg
Pinch of ground black pepper
1 x 185g (6½oz) tin tuna (in
    spring water) – drained
30g (1¼oz) medium Cheddar
    cheese – grated

Cook the macaroni according to the packet instructions. Once cooked, drain and set aside.

Tomato masala: Heat the oil in a frying pan, add the onion and stir-fry on medium-low heat for 2 mins until soft. Add the garlic, ginger, tomato and oregano and stir-fry for a few mins until the tomato chunks begin to soften, then set aside.

White sauce: In a pot, melt the butter on low heat and spoon in the flour. Stir continuously until a paste is formed, then pour in the milk, a little at a time, and whisk vigorously to avoid any lumps appearing. Once all of the milk has been poured in, add the nutmeg and black pepper and flake in the tuna. Bring to the boil on low heat and simmer (uncovered) for 4–5 mins, stirring occasionally. Once cooked, add the cheese and the tomato masala to the sauce and stir. If the sauce looks very heavy, add some extra milk.

Toss the cooked macaroni into the sauce and combine well. Serve to baby warm.

Indian Salmon Risotto

Salmon contains all of the Super Food health benefits of oily fish, and encompasses another major one, being rich in vitamin D – the 'Sunshine Vitamin'. Essential for building strong muscles and bones (by regulating calcium in the body), this vitamin is vital for helping your little one learn to walk. Although the best source of vitamin D is the sunshine, this mouth-watering textured risotto will add an extra little boost into her diet.

6 servings | up to 35 mins

1 tbsp olive oil
1 small onion – peeled, chopped
¼ tsp minced ginger
½ tsp minced garlic
Pinch of ground nutmeg
Pinch of ground cumin
Pinch of ground black pepper
1 curry leaf
100g (3½oz) Arborio risotto rice – washed, drained
750ml (1¼ pints) hot vegetable or fish stock – baby-friendly
60g (2½oz) parsnip – washed, peeled, cubed
60g (2½oz) broccoli florets – washed, chopped (no stems)
1 x 100g (3½oz) salmon fillet (skinless, boneless)
1 tsp unsalted butter – softened
2 tbsp whole milk

Heat the oil in a pot, add the onion and stir-fry for 4–5 mins until golden. Then add the ginger, garlic and all of the spices and lightly cook for 30 secs–1 min. Add the rice and stock to the pot, stir and bring to the boil. Simmer (covered) on low heat for 15–20 mins until creamy and tender.

While the rice is cooking, steam the parsnip and broccoli in a steamer, or in the microwave by placing them in a microwavable dish and adding 2 tablespoons of water. Cover the dish with either a lid (leaving a small vent) or cling film (piercing a few holes), and steam on high for 1½–2 mins until tender. Once cooked, drain and set aside.

Next place the salmon in a microwavable dish, gently rub in the butter and spoon over the milk. Poach in the microwave (covered, leaving a small vent) for 2–3 mins until the fish is flaky. Check halfway through to ensure the fish does not overcook.

Once the rice is cooked, add the steamed veggies and flake in the salmon, ensuring there are no sneaky bones left. Combine together for a delicious, aromatic meal.

Finger Food Super Meals

Stage 2 | 7 Months Plus
Stage 3 | 10 Months Plus

Finger foods are bite-size or stick-shaped pieces of food babies can pick up with their podgy little fingers to feed themselves with, known as baby-led weaning or self-feeding. Great for baby's hand to eye co-ordination and for her independence, so should be encouraged with lots of enthusiastic clapping and cheering from mummy and daddy.

The other benefits of self-feeding include healthier eating habits as babies develop a positive relationship with picking up and eating healthy foods, and weight control. Self-fed babies are in control of their own appetite so they are more likely to be a healthier weight over spoon-fed babies.

I chose to use both spoon-feeding and self-feeding techniques with Aaliyah. Spoon-feeding was adopted at main meal times whereas self-feeding was encouraged at snack times. I found this routine worked perfectly for us; for me, as I knew Aaliyah had eaten well; for Aaliyah, to practise her pincer grip, allowing her to perfect her motor skills.

'Gummy babies' can still eat finger foods. Just be certain the food you have prepared can be mushed easily between little gums and will melt-in-the-mouth.

If your little one is not exploring food with her hands or self-feeding at 7 months, she will at some point. So I would recommend investing in some long-sleeved bibs and plastic mats (or throw down a towel) for the floor as things are going to get very messy!

Please be vigilant when babies are self-feeding as finger foods are a choking hazard. Babies should be supervised at all times.

Appleberry French Toast

A delicious soft, fluffy, finger food made with a fruity blend of naturally sweet apple juice combined with the popular Super Food blueberries. In addition to their well-known antioxidant power, blueberries are great for eye health, improving memory, and maintaining healthy bones through their vitamin K, calcium and zinc content.

40g (1½oz) blueberries –
   fresh, washed
1 egg yolk (optional)
100ml (3½fl oz) whole milk
50ml (2fl oz) pure unsweetened
   apple juice
Sprinkle of ground cinnamon
2 slices of bread – white
2 knobs of unsalted butter

Add the blueberries, egg yolk (if using), milk, apple juice and cinnamon to a blender and blend until smooth. Then pour the mixture into a dish large enough to dip a slice of bread in.

Place one slice of bread in the dish, face down, and let it soak for a few secs without letting it get soggy. Turn it over and repeat on the other side.

Heat one knob of butter in a frying pan and gently place the slice of bread in. Cook on medium heat for a few mins until golden brown, then repeat on the other side. If you are using egg, you must ensure both sides are cooked thoroughly.

Once cooked, cut the french toast into strips or bite-size pieces and serve to baby warm. Repeat the process for the second slice of bread.

Tip: for an authentic French toast recipe, remove the blueberries and apple juice and replace them with a few drops of vanilla.

Minted Green Beans

Naturally grown in a handy finger food shape, green beans are bursting with nutrients. They contain antioxidant vitamins A and C for bone health, and vitamin K which is necessary for blood-clotting to heal cuts and wounds effectively.

250ml (8fl oz) hot vegetable stock – baby-friendly
Pinch of dried mint
Pinch of ground nutmeg
80g (3oz) green beans – washed, ends chopped off, halved

Pour the stock into a pot, add the mint and nutmeg and bring to the boil.

Then add the green beans to the stock and simmer (uncovered) on medium heat for 5–6 mins until the beans are tender.

Once cooked, remove the beans from the pot, drain (discarding the stock), and serve to baby warm on its own, or with my Mint Yogurt Raita (page 109) as a tasty dip.

Tip: When you are cooking with fresh green beans, test the freshness by 'snapping' one before you buy as the 'snap' is the sign of a healthy bean.

Sweet Egg Curry

Served as a delicious lunch or dinner, this excellent protein-rich meal is chock-full of Super Spice goodness. It incorporates a range of health benefits from the spices including anti-bacterial protection (turmeric), preventative treatment against dry skin and eczema (coriander), and healthy digestion and bowels (from all of the spices).

1 egg
1 tbsp whole milk
Pinch of ground black pepper
1½ tsp olive oil
½ onion – peeled, chopped
½ tomato – washed,
   deseeded, finely chopped
¼ tsp minced ginger
¼ tsp minced garlic
Pinch of ground turmeric
Pinch of ground coriander
½ banana – peeled, cubed

Crack the egg into a bowl, spoon in the milk, add the black pepper and whisk. Then set aside.

Heat the oil in a frying pan, add the onion and stir-fry on low heat for 2 mins until golden. Then add the tomato, ginger, garlic, turmeric and coriander and cook for 2 mins until the tomato is soft.

Pour the whisked egg into the frying pan and stir-fry on low heat until the egg is well-cooked and light and fluffy in texture. Pop the banana into the frying pan and stir-fry for a few secs.

Allow to cool before serving to baby as a yummy, squidgy finger food. Or for older babies, serve with roti for a more filling meal.

Tip: for a savoury taste, omit the banana.

Warm Buttery Pitta Bread

Popular in Middle-Eastern, Mediterranean and Indian cuisines, pitta bread is a quick, healthy snack to provide your little one with a whole grain boost between meals. The complex carbohydrates in the pitta ensure energy is released slowly to keep her going until her next meal time.

1 wholemeal pitta bread – ready-made
Knob of unsalted butter or ghee

Place the pitta bread in the toaster for 2–3 mins until warm, but not crispy. Alternatively, warm it under the grill, or in the oven or microwave.

Then lay the pitta on a plate and spread the butter or ghee over it. Cut into slices and serve to baby on its own.

For older babies, serve with my Aubergine Bharta (Dip) on page 93. Also delicious served with any of my curries as an alternative to roti.

Seasoned Sweet Potato Fries

If your little one is teething, this tasty snack may help to sooth those uncomfortable symptoms. The nutmeg not only provides a warm, aromatic taste to complement the sweet potato, it also contains the compound 'eugenol', which is used as a natural medicine to treat toothaches. Combined with the powerful analgesic properties of cinnamon, this is a wonderful snack to combat teething pains.

1½ tsp olive oil
¼ tsp ground cinnamon
Pinch of ground nutmeg
1 small sweet potato –
  washed, peeled, cut
  into 5cm (2in) sticks

Preheat the oven to 200°C/400°F/gas mark 6.

Put the oil, cinnamon and nutmeg in a bowl and stir. Add the potato sticks and give them a good toss to coat with the seasoning. Lay them flat on a foil-covered baking tray and place on the middle shelf of the oven.

Bake for 20–25 mins or until tender, turning over halfway through. Allow to cool before serving to baby.

Roti Sticks

Yummy! Freshly made home-cooked rotis (chapattis) are delicious, soft and melt-in-the-mouth. Aaliyah loved eating them either on their own, or smeared with a little unsalted butter and a tiny sprinkling of ground cinnamon. Roti is a wonderful healthy snack for your baby. Being a starchy food, it provides your little one with lots of energy for playing and moving around.

150g (5oz) wholemeal chapatti/atta flour, plus extra for sprinkling
1 tbsp vegetable oil
250ml (8fl oz) hot water
Unsalted butter, to serve

Place the flour and oil in a bowl and add the water a little at a time, stirring. Continue adding water until a soft (but not sticky) dough ball is formed. Then remove the dough ball from the bowl and knead for 1–2 mins.

Divide the dough into 8 pieces and shape into small round balls. Sprinkle some flour over the counter and rolling pin so the dough doesn't stick, and roll out one of the balls until it resembles a flat, round 25cm (10in) pancake. Repeat this process for all the dough balls.

Heat a large frying pan or thava (round, flat frying pan) until hot, and cook one roti on medium heat until bubbles appear on the surface and the roti begins to brown. Turn it over and cook until bubbles appear on the other side. Then flip the roti at regular intervals until it begins to puff up. Remove and set aside. Repeat for all the rotis.

Once cooked, spread a little unsalted butter over the fresh roti, cut into strips and serve immediately while still warm. Alternatively, you can freeze the rotis for later. See page 188 for storage details.

Scrambled Egg with Cheese and Onion

An excellent high-quality protein meal, ensuring your little one receives at least one of her 2-a-day portions from the protein-rich food group. Served as a delicious breakfast, this will be a great start to her day.

1 tbsp olive oil
½ onion – peeled, chopped
1 egg
1 tbsp whole milk
Pinch of ground black pepper
7g (¼oz) medium Cheddar
   cheese – grated

Heat the oil in a frying pan, add the onion and stir-fry on medium-low heat for 2 mins until golden. While the onion is cooking, crack the egg into a bowl, add the milk and black pepper and whisk.

Once the onion is cooked, turn to low heat and add the egg mixture to the pan. Gently stir-fry the egg until it is cooked to a soft, fluffy texture. Switch off the heat and sprinkle over the cheese. Fold it in until it melts and is combined well with the egg.

Serve to baby once cooled as a tasty, squidgy finger food. For older babies, serve with roti or buttered toast as a delicious breakfast.

Aubergine Bharta (Dip)

Originally from Punjab, this yummy flavoursome dip can be served as a very messy finger food. The deep plum-coloured Super Food, aubergine, is bursting with nutrients. A great source of fibre and B vitamins and potassium, which is excellent for heart health.

4 baby aubergines –
  washed, pricked all over
1 tbsp olive oil
½ onion – peeled, chopped
1 tomato – washed,
  deseeded, chopped
½ tsp minced garlic
Pinch of ground cumin
Pinch of ground coriander
Pinch of ground black pepper
1 tbsp plain unsweetened
  yogurt

Preheat the oven to 200°C/400°F/gas mark 6. Place the aubergines on a baking tray and bake for 15–20 mins until soft to the touch. Cool.

While the aubergines are baking, heat the oil in a pot, add the onion and stir-fry on low heat for 3–4 mins. Add the tomato, garlic, cumin, coriander and black pepper and stir-fry on medium heat until the juice from the tomato has cooked away and the flesh is very soft.

Turn to low heat and add the yogurt a little at a time, stirring continuously to avoid curdling. Stir-fry for a further min, then set aside.

Once the aubergines are cooked and cooled, cut them in half lengthways and scoop out the flesh; it should be juicy and soft. Add the flesh to the pot with the cooked onion and tomato and combine. Mash or blend to achieve a textured paste. Serve to baby warm with wholemeal pitta bread strips.

Tip: the best way to cook an aubergine is to bake it. There's better flavour, it's juicier and for us mums; it's hassle-free! Whack it in the oven, have a cuppa until the oven bleeps.

Banana and Cinnamon Roti Wrap

A roti wrap, also called a 'baaboro' in my home, was my favourite childhood snack. My mum would cook soft, fresh melt-in-the-mouth rotis. They'd be smeared with ghee, sprinkled with sugar, rolled and scoffed. It was delicious! My version is just as delicious but far more nutritious for baby. Prepared with potassium-rich bananas and immune-strengthening sweet cinnamon, this version will be scoffed just as quickly!

1 roti – homemade (page 88)
  or ready-made
1 tsp unsalted butter or ghee
Sprinkle of ground cinnamon
1 banana – peeled, sliced

Warm the roti in a large frying pan, in the microwave on high for 10–20 secs, or on a thava (round, flat frying pan), if you have one.

Once warmed, spread the butter or ghee evenly over the roti and lightly sprinkle the cinnamon over it. Add the banana slices in a row, roll up the roti and cut into bite-size pieces for your little one.

Tip one: this 5-minute Super Meal is also fabulous as a quick after-school snack for older children.

Tip two: make this finger food suitable for Stage 2 babies by offering the slices of banana without the roti, and just a touch of cinnamon.

Playdate Pizza Pitta Fingers

Dried mixed herbs are fantastic! Thyme, parsley, oregano, sage and basil – some of the most highly ranked Super Spices, all available in one handy jar. This combination ensures your little one will receive vitamins A and K, iron and anti-bacterial and anti-inflammatory protection, all sprinkled into a delicious tomato sauce, which is also rich in lycopene.

Tomato sauce base:
1 x 400g (14oz) tin chopped
  tomatoes
1 tsp minced garlic
½ tsp dried mixed herbs
¼ tsp ground cumin
Pinch of ground black pepper

1 pack of 6 standard (oval)
  pittas – white or wholemeal
40g (1½oz) medium Cheddar
  cheese – grated

One serving:
1–2 tbsp tomato sauce base
1 pitta – white or wholemeal
Handful of grated medium
  Cheddar cheese

Pop the tomatoes, garlic, herbs, cumin and black pepper into a pot and simmer on medium-low heat until well-cooked, and the sauce thickens. Then set aside.

Lay all of the pittas on a foil-covered baking tray and distribute the tomato sauce evenly between all six. Sprinkle over the cheese, then place them under a hot grill until the cheese has melted and is bubbling. Remove from the grill, then cut into long strips. Leave to cool before serving to baby and friends.

One serving: It is more convenient to cook up a big batch of tomato sauce base in one go rather than cooking just enough for one serving, so follow the same method as above, and then freeze the remaining sauce into individual servings (page 189).

Tip: add mushrooms, sweetcorn and red peppers and transform this finger food into a quick and filling after-school snack for older children.

Sweet Super Meals

Stage 2 | 7 Months Plus
Stage 3 | 10 Months Plus

When describing Asian desserts, the words rich, luscious and indulgent come to mind.

A few other words come to mind too: unhealthy, sugary and saturated fats!

Nevertheless, knowing all too well how delicious Asian desserts are, I was not going to let Aaliyah miss out on these delights! So taste was definitely one of the biggest influences behind creating these wonderful puddings for her. The other stemmed from 'my big fat family gatherings'. While everyone indulged in mithai (sweets), gajar halwa, seviyan and more at family events, Aaliyah would sit and watch every mouthful her uncles, aunts and cousins devoured, completely mesmerised. I felt awful, like a wicked witch who wouldn't let her daughter enjoy these wonderful desserts.

So this chapter is dedicated to healthy adaptations of traditional Asian desserts exclusively for baby to indulge in. The words to describe these desserts are: energy-boosting, probiotic, fresh fruity goodness, naturally sweet and fibre-rich.

Being exceptionally nutritious, these desserts can also be served as healthy snacks, and for as long as your little one wants to enjoy them for. Aaliyah still adored these desserts at 18 months and beyond, so there really is no strict time frame on these recipes.

Bananaberry Raita

A delicious, naturally sweet fresh fruit raita that Aaliyah still adores! This one is a Super Food and Super Spice bonanza because every ingredient has amazing health benefits. Yogurt is probiotic and calcium-rich and the potassium (in bananas) works efficiently to aid calcium absorption, leading to strong teeth and bones for baby. The blueberries add an extra boost of vitamins C and K, and the ginger keeps the digestive tract in healthy working order.

1 banana – peeled, sliced
Handful of blueberries –
   fresh, washed, halved
2–3 tbsp plain unsweetened
   yogurt
Sprinkle of ground ginger

Place the banana and blueberries in a bowl, spoon in the yogurt and sprinkle over the ginger.

Mash the fruit with a spoon to create soft lumps for baby, and stir. The yogurt will change colour from white to a very subtle shade of purple, courtesy of the blueberries.

Serve to baby as a dessert, or a healthy between-meals snack.

Classic Gajar Halwa

Gajar Halwa – a famous Indian dessert. The key ingredient is the Super Food, carrot, so you know this dish is bursting with beta-carotene goodness. Raisins, if consumed in moderation, have fab health benefits of their own as they are rich in antioxidants and are a good source of iron, potassium and energy.

1 tbsp unsalted butter or ghee
1 whole cardamom pod – green
2 medium carrots – washed, peeled, grated (in a food processor)
150ml (¼ pint) whole milk
Pinch of ground cinnamon
15g (½oz) raisins – soaked in warm water (5 mins), drained, chopped

Melt the butter or ghee in a pot, add the cardamom pod and carrots and stir-fry for 5 mins.

Pour in the milk and add the cinnamon and raisins. Bring to the boil gradually on a low heat; this will take 5–10 mins.

Simmer (uncovered) for 15 mins, stirring occasionally until the mixture begins to thicken. Once all of the milk has been absorbed, remove from the heat. Serve to baby warm.

IMPORTANT: remove the cardamom pod before serving to baby.

Coconut Seviyan (Vermicelli Pudding)

Traditionally served as either breakfast or dessert, seviyan (vermicelli) is deliciously creamy. Made from very thin pasta, this dish is an excellent starchy food source for baby. The complex carbohydrates combined with the energy-boosting power of the coconut makes this a perfect slow release energy snack.

1 tbsp unsalted butter or ghee
40g (1½oz) vermicelli
350ml (12fl oz) whole milk
3 saffron strands
1 tbsp unsweetened
   desiccated coconut
15g (½oz) raisins – soaked
   in warm water (5 mins),
   drained, chopped

Melt the butter or ghee in a pot. Over the pot, break the vermicelli into small pieces with your hands and toss in. Stir-fry lightly on low heat for 2–3 mins until it turns golden brown.

Pour in the milk and add the saffron, coconut and raisins. Bring to the boil gradually on low heat; this will take 5–10 mins. Simmer (uncovered) until the milk becomes creamy, but still remains fluid, stirring occasionally.

If the seviyan becomes too thick, add some extra milk, stir and serve to baby while warm. Delicious!

Creamy Sweet Potato Dream

This warm, sweet, aromatic delight is yummy and bursting with immune-boosting capabilities, supplied by beta-carotene (vitamin A) found in the sweet potato, and the lauric acid found in the coconut milk.

1 medium sweet potato –
    washed, peeled, finely sliced
200ml (7fl oz) unsweetened
    coconut milk
150ml (¼ pint) whole milk
Sprinkle of ground nutmeg
1 whole cardamom pod – green

Place the sweet potato slices in a layer at the bottom of a large pot. Continue to layer until all of the slices have been used up, and cover with the coconut milk and whole milk.

Bring to the boil gradually on low heat; this will take 5–10 mins. Then simmer (covered) for 10 mins or until the potatoes are thoroughly cooked. Remove from the heat and mash. The milk will transform to a light orange colour and the consistency should be quite runny. If not, add some extra milk.

Return to the heat, adding the nutmeg and cardamom pod and stir. Simmer (uncovered) on low heat for a further 5–10 mins until the milk thickens. Once cooked, serve to baby warm.

IMPORTANT: remove the cardamom pod before serving to baby.

Mint Yogurt Raita

It's not sweet, I know, but this seemed like the most appropriate place to put it! Yogurt raitas are a common accompaniment to Indian dishes – they go together like fish and chips! For Aaliyah, I created this savoury raita to add another layer of flavour to my curries and to get an extra probiotic boost into her diet. The 'good' bacteria from the yogurt, combined with the digestive power of the mint, cumin and ginger, suggests healthy bowels all round.

2 tbsp plain unsweetened
   yogurt
¼ tsp dried mint
Sprinkle of ground cumin
Sprinkle of ground ginger

Spoon the yogurt into a bowl and add the mint, cumin and ginger. Fold the aromatic spices into the yogurt until well combined.

Serve alongside any of my curries in this book.

Papaya Shrikhand (Yogurt)

A traditional sweet yogurt dessert chock-full of probiotic goodness, containing the exotic, golden orange Super Food, papaya. Filled with antioxidants, papaya is great for eye health, a healthy immune system, wound-healing, digestion and asthma prevention.

½ tbsp whole milk
2 saffron strands
4 tbsp plain unsweetened
    yogurt
½ ripe papaya – peeled,
    deseeded, cubed
Pinch of ground cardamom –
    green

Pour the milk into a cup, warm for a few secs on high in the microwave, add the saffron, stir and set aside. The warm milk will help the saffron to dissolve. When this happens, the milk will slowly transform from white to a light golden orange colour.

Next spoon the yogurt into a blender and add the papaya, cardamom and orange saffron milk. Blend until smooth, then place in a small container and serve to baby.

Tip: this is also delicious prepared with mango, with the same beta-carotene goodness!

Saffron Date Kheer (Rice Pudding)

A luscious, creamy, gorgeous rice pudding! Even I've had a few sneaky mouthfuls of this one. Containing saffron, the world's most expensive spice, it's believed to be anti-cancer and great for eyes and the immune system. Dates are also impressive! This delicious fruit is a concentrated source of energy, fibre-rich, helping to keep bowels healthy, and a wonderful source of minerals – potassium, calcium, iron and zinc.

40g (1½oz) white basmati rice
 – washed, drained
600ml (1 pint) whole milk
3 saffron strands
Sprinkle of ground cinnamon
15g (½oz) fresh dates –
 stoned, finely chopped

Place the rice in a pot, pour in half of the milk and stir (you will need to save the rest for later).

Bring the milk and rice to the boil gradually on low heat; this will take 5–10 mins. Let it simmer (uncovered) until all of the milk has been absorbed by the rice. It will be thick and creamy.

Remove from the heat and mash the rice. Return to the heat and pour in the remaining milk. Add the saffron, cinnamon and dates and stir. Simmer (uncovered) on low heat until the milk and mashed rice have combined into a rich, gooey consistency. If the kheer becomes too thick, just add some extra milk and stir.

Serve to baby warm as an after meal treat.

Apple and Pear Jardo (Sweet Rice)

Growing up I've always loved this sweet rice dessert. The rice was cooked in tons of sugar and it was bright orange in colour! There really was nothing healthy about it but it tasted amazing! However, my reinvented version for baby ensures the sweet taste comes from natural sources – tender apple and pear chunks. Combined with the whole grain goodness of rice, this jardo is chock-full of fibre and complex carbohydrates, providing your little one with lots of slow release energy to keep her playing for longer.

1 tbsp unsalted butter or ghee
1 tbsp vegetable oil
1 small cinnamon stick
1 whole cardamom pod – green
400ml (14fl oz) water
100ml (3½fl oz) pure unsweetened apple juice
100g (3½oz) brown basmati rice – soaked in water (10 mins), washed, drained
½ sweet apple – peeled, cored, chopped
1 small firm pear – peeled, cored, chopped

Heat the butter or ghee and oil in a pot on low heat and add the cinnamon stick and cardamom pod. Stir-fry for a min then pour in the water and apple juice and add the rice. Bring to the boil and simmer (covered) for 35–40 mins until all of the liquid has been absorbed and the rice is tender.

While the rice is cooking, steam the apple and pear in a steamer, or in the microwave by placing them in a microwavable dish and adding 2 tablespoons of water. Cover the dish with either a lid (leaving a small vent) or cling film (piercing a few holes), and steam on high for 1–1½ mins until tender.

Once cooked, drain off the excess water and add the fruit chunks to the cooked rice. Combine well. Serve to baby warm as a dessert or healthy snack... yummy!

IMPORTANT: remove the cinnamon stick and cardamom pod before serving to baby.

Mango and Banana Lassi

Lassi, a scrumptious traditional yogurt-based drink, typically loaded with sugar. Baby's version, however, is not, and is comparable to a fruit smoothie. As with banana, mango provides a vast range of health benefits, too. Believed to prevent asthma and cancer, it also promotes healthy bowels and bones, and is fabulous for healthy eyes and skin and luscious hair.

4 tbsp plain unsweetened yogurt
½ ripe mango – peeled, stoned, cubed
½ banana – peeled, halved

Place the yogurt, mango and banana into a blender and blend until smooth. Pour into baby's drinking/sippy cup and serve.

Alternative fruit lassi combinations include:

❋ Sweet Plum and Blueberry Lassi

❋ Papaya and Mango Lassi

❋ Strawberry and Raspberry Lassi

Feel free to get creative and try out new and exciting fruit combinations, so you can tailor them specifically to your little one's taste buds.

Meat Super Meals

By this stage, your little one will be a well-oiled chewing machine. This newly perfected skill will allow her to break down meat effectively, making it easier for her digestive system to process it. So if you have already introduced meat into baby's diet, there is no longer any need to purée the meat before serving.

If you are just about to introduce meat, however, chicken is a great place to start! In addition, cook with lean cuts of meat, as lots of fat will be difficult for baby to digest. Try to use the following cuts:

Chicken – skinless, boneless breast portions
Turkey – skinless, boneless breast portions
Lamb – stew/casserole meat chunks
Beef – top sirloin or eye of round roast

When I embarked on Aaliyah's meat and poultry journey from the age of 10 months, I offered her lean minced meat meals to begin with, either chicken or lamb, as the meat was already ground into tiny pieces. I then moved on to small tender chunks of meat, shredding cooked chunks with my fingers before serving. As Aaliyah grew, I left the small chunks whole and she would shred or cut them herself, usually with her one tooth!

At this stage, I was also more confident with the food I was feeding Aaliyah. So these Super Meals are chunkier, include new spices, and are a step closer to big family meals.

IMPORTANT: you must ensure ALL meat and poultry has been thoroughly cooked to avoid food poisoning.

Classic Keema Curry

A mouth-watering traditional curry perfect as a first meat dish for baby. An excellent mixture of essential amino acids for healthy growth, starch for energy and yummy bright green antioxidant peas. Cook this curry with any meat you like! Minced chicken, lamb or beef are all good – using different meats will alter the taste of this curry considerably.

2 tbsp olive oil
1 onion – peeled, chopped
1 whole clove
1 whole black peppercorn
1 small cinnamon stick
1 tsp minced ginger
1 tsp minced garlic
100g (3½oz) lean lamb, beef or chicken mince
1 tomato – washed, deseeded, grated
½ tsp ground cumin
½ tsp ground coriander
¼ tsp ground turmeric
1½ tsp tomato purée
1 small white potato – washed, peeled, cubed
40g (1½oz) peas – frozen, washed

Heat the oil in a pot and add the onion, clove, peppercorn and cinnamon stick. Stir-fry on medium heat until the onion is golden. Add the ginger and garlic and stir-fry for a further 30 secs–1 min and then add the mince and continue to stir-fry until the meat is sealed. Add the tomato, cumin, coriander, turmeric and tomato purée, stir-fry for a further min, then turn to low heat, add a splash of water and simmer (covered) for 10–15 mins or until the mince is thoroughly cooked.

While the mince is cooking, place the potato cubes in a microwavable dish and add 2 tablespoons of water. Cover the dish with either a lid (leaving a small vent) or cling film (piercing a few holes), and steam on high for 2–2½ mins until tender. Drain and set aside.

Once the mince mixture is cooked, add the peas to the pot, stir and continue to simmer (covered) for 2–3 mins until the peas are tender. Switch off the heat, add the potato cubes and combine well. Serve to baby warm with roti and a dollop of plain yogurt. Delicious!

IMPORTANT: remove the clove, black peppercorn and cinnamon stick before serving to baby.

Chicken and Saag Pasanda

By far one of Aaliyah's favourite meals! Spinach (saag), a dark leafy green Super Food, is great for healthy eyes and boosting immunity, and is a good source of iron and vitamin K – essential for bone health. When teamed with protein-rich chicken, it makes a fabulously nutritious curry. Chicken contains selenium, believed to be anti-cancer, and it is key for a healthy metabolism.

6 servings   25 mins

2 tbsp olive oil
1 onion – peeled, chopped
1 small cinnamon stick
½ tsp minced ginger
½ tsp minced garlic
1 chicken breast fillet
    (skinless) – cut into 1cm
    (½in) cubes
¼ tsp ground turmeric
150ml (¼ pint) water
½ tsp ground garam masala
1 tbsp tomato purée
3 tbsp plain unsweetened
    yogurt
125g (4oz) spinach leaves –
    washed thoroughly,
    chopped (no stems)

Heat the oil in a pot, add the onion and cinnamon stick and stir-fry on medium-low heat for 3–4 mins. Then add the ginger, garlic, chicken and turmeric. Stir-fry for a min, then turn to low heat, add the water, garam masala, tomato purée and the yogurt, one spoon at a time, stirring in-between to avoid curdling. Simmer (uncovered) on low heat for 8–10 mins until the chicken is tender.

While the chicken is simmering, steam the spinach using a steamer, or in the microwave by placing it in a microwavable dish (do not add any water); cover the dish with either a lid (leaving a small vent) or cling film (piercing a few holes), and steam on high for 2½ mins or until wilted. Drain off the excess water and set aside.

Once the chicken is tender, add the cooked spinach and combine well. Cut or shred the chicken cubes as necessary and serve to baby warm with roti or overcooked mushy rice.

IMPORTANT: remove the cinnamon stick before serving to baby.

Chicken Pilaf with Vegetables

Pilaf, a traditional rice dish cooked with either vegetables, meat or both. Yogurt plays an important role in this dish, acting as a wonderful substitute for salt by providing a tangy taste to the meal. It is also a great source of calcium, potassium and protein (as well as the chicken). Chicken has the added benefit of selenium and being rich in B vitamins, both necessary for converting food into energy.

6 servings 25 mins

1½ tbsp olive oil
1 onion – peeled, chopped
1 whole cardamom pod – black
1 whole clove
1 small cinnamon stick
1 tomato – washed,
  deseeded, chopped
¼ tsp ground black pepper
1 tsp cumin seeds
1 tsp minced ginger
1 tsp minced garlic
Juice of ½ lemon – ensuring
  no seeds fall in
2 tbsp plain unsweetened
  yogurt
1 chicken breast fillet
  (skinless) – cut into 1cm
  (½in) cubes
100g (3½oz) white basmati
  rice – washed, drained
60g (2½oz) cauliflower florets
  – washed, chopped
  (no stems)
250ml (8fl oz) water
40g (1½oz) peas – frozen,
  washed

Heat the oil in a pot and add the onion, cardamom pod, clove and cinnamon stick. Stir-fry until the onion browns. Turn to low heat and add the tomato, black pepper, cumin seeds, ginger, garlic, lemon juice and yogurt, one spoon at a time, stirring in-between to avoid curdling. Then add the chicken and stir-fry for 5 mins.

Add the rice and cauliflower to the pot, pour in the water, stir and bring to the boil. Simmer (covered) on low heat for 10–15 mins until the rice is tender and all the water is absorbed.

While the rice is cooking, steam the peas in a steamer, or in the microwave by placing them in a microwavable dish and adding 2 tablespoons of water. Cover the dish with either a lid (leaving a small vent) or cling film (piercing a few holes), and steam on high for 1–1½ mins. Drain and set aside.

Once the rice is tender (it will look a little moist when it's done), add the peas, combine well, cover the pot and set aside for 5 mins. Serve to baby warm.

IMPORTANT: remove the cardamom pod, clove and cinnamon stick before serving to baby.

Chunky Spaghetti Bolognaise

Aaliyah loved this Super Meal, she slurped up the lot in record time! Containing the Super Food apricot, this fruit is fibre-rich and loaded with beta-carotene. The bolognaise sauce also includes dried oregano, a Super Spice containing one of the highest antioxidant levels compared to other Super Spices (see page 14). Oregano is anti-bacterial, great for toothache, and loaded with vitamin K, which is required for effective blood clotting to heal wounds and for building strong bones.

6 servings | up to 25 mins

2 tbsp olive oil
1 onion – peeled, chopped
1 tsp minced garlic
½ tsp minced ginger
100g (3½oz) lean lamb, beef or chicken mince
Pinch of ground black pepper
½ tsp ground garam masala
¼ tsp ground turmeric
1 x 200g (7oz) tin chopped tomatoes
200ml (7fl oz) water
1 medium carrot – washed, peeled, grated
1 small courgette – washed, grated
25g (1oz) dried apricots – finely chopped
¼ tsp dried oregano
1 tbsp tomato purée

Heat the oil in a pot, add the onion and stir-fry on medium-low heat for 3–4 mins until soft and golden. Add the garlic and ginger and stir-fry for 30 secs–1 min, then add the mince along with the black pepper, garam masala and turmeric and stir-fry until the meat is sealed. Add the tomatoes and pour in half of the water (you will need to save the rest for later). Simmer (covered) on low heat for 5–6 mins.

Finally add the carrot, courgette, apricots, oregano, tomato purée and the remaining water. Continue to simmer for a further 10 mins until the mince and all of the vegetables are well-cooked.

One serving: Serve 2–3 heaped tablespoons of bolognaise sauce with 20g (¾oz) cooked spaghetti, broken into small pieces.

Save the remaining sauce by freezing it in individual servings (page 189). Then simply boil up enough spaghetti for one serving every time you take a bolognaise portion out of the freezer.

Garam Yorkshire Hotpot

A traditional slow-cooked meal originating from the north of England. This is a hearty hotpot with a little garam masala thrown in for good measure. Loaded with iron, zinc, protein, and selenium for baby, this meal is delicious and nutritious.

25g (1oz) unsalted butter
100g (3½oz) lean lamb cubes
  – boneless, fat-trimmed,
  cut into 1cm (½in) pieces
Sprinkle of plain flour
1 tbsp olive oil
½ onion – peeled, chopped
1 medium carrot – washed,
  peeled, grated
1 bay leaf
¼ tsp minced garlic
¼ tsp ground garam masala
4 tbsp lamb stock – baby-
  friendly
1 white potato – washed,
  peeled, sliced
Melted unsalted butter or
  extra olive oil, for brushing

Preheat oven to 160°C/325°F/gas mark 3.

Melt the butter in a frying pan and add the lamb and flour. Stir-fry continuously until the lamb pieces have browned. Then remove and place in a small ovenproof dish.

In the same frying pan, heat the oil, then add the onion, carrot and bay leaf and stir-fry until the onion is soft and golden. Add the garlic and garam masala to the pan and stir-fry for a further 30 secs, then immediately pour the mixture over the lamb in the ovenproof dish, followed by the stock. Place the potato slices in a layer over the top to form a cover for the stew underneath.

Brush a little melted butter or extra oil over the potato slices, cover the dish loosely with foil, place on the middle shelf of the oven and slow cook for 1½ hours.

Leave to cool and shred or mash the meal as necessary for baby. Serve to baby warm. For older children, serve with a side of freshly cooked vegetables for a more filling meal.

IMPORTANT: remove the bay leaf before serving to baby.

Coconut Chicken Curry

This Super Meal is bursting with immune-strengthening ingredients. Fresh lemon and broccoli provide vitamin C, and the coconut provides a source of anti-viral fats to keep cold and flu viruses at bay. In addition, the chicken is an excellent source of 'essential' amino acids (protein), required for healthy growth and development.

8 servings   25 mins

1½ tbsp olive oil
1 onion – peeled, chopped
1 chicken breast fillet
    (skinless) – cut into 1cm
    (½in) cubes
¼ tsp ground turmeric
1 tomato – washed,
    deseeded, grated
½ tsp minced garlic
¼ tsp ground cumin
150ml (¼ pint) unsweetened
    coconut milk
1 tbsp unsweetened
    desiccated coconut
Juice of ½ lemon – ensuring
    no seeds fall in
¼ tsp ground garam masala
60g (2½oz) broccoli florets –
    washed, chopped (no stems)

Heat the oil in a pot, add the onion and stir-fry on medium-low heat for 3–4 mins until soft and golden. Add the chicken and turmeric and stir-fry until the chicken is sealed. Add the tomato, garlic and cumin and continue to stir-fry for a further 2–3 mins.

Add the coconut milk, desiccated coconut, lemon juice and garam masala and simmer on low heat for a further 10 mins, stirring occasionally until the chicken is tender. If at any point the curry looks dry, add a little water and continue to simmer.

While the chicken is simmering, steam the broccoli in a steamer, or in the microwave by placing it in a microwavable dish and adding 2 tablespoons of water. Cover the dish with either a lid (leaving a small vent) or cling film (piercing a few holes), and steam on high for 1½–2 mins until tender. Once cooked, drain off the excess water and add to the curry at the end. Combine well and serve to baby warm with roti or overcooked mushy rice.

Fruity Lamb Tagine

A heavenly tagine so delicious I often make a family size portion and serve it up as a main meal. Incredibly easy to make, protein-rich and abundant in vitamins and minerals, this tagine is a real gem. The paprika in this scrumptious meal can increase your little one's iron intake, along with vitamin E, for healthy skin and eyes. Equally impressive, the apricots provide vitamin A (beta-carotene), and the tomatoes are a source of vitamin C and antioxidant lycopene.

1 tbsp olive oil
1 onion – peeled, chopped
1 tsp minced garlic
200g (7oz) lean lamb (boneless) – cut into 1cm (½in) cubes
Sprinkle of plain flour
1 x 200g (7oz) tin chopped tomatoes
450ml (16fl oz) vegetable or lamb stock – baby-friendly
Juice of ½ lemon – ensuring no seeds fall in
1 small cinnamon stick
½ tsp ground cumin
½ tsp ground coriander
¼ tsp ground black pepper
½ tsp ground paprika
½ tsp ground ginger
20g (¾oz) raisins
50g (2oz) dried apricots – finely chopped
1 firm pear – peeled, cored, sliced

Heat the oil in a large pot, add the onion and garlic and stir-fry on medium-low heat until the onion is soft and golden. Then add the lamb and flour and stir-fry for a few mins until the lamb has browned.

Pour in the tomatoes, stock and lemon juice, then add all the spices (cinnamon stick, cumin, coriander, black pepper, paprika and ginger) and all of the fruit (raisins, apricots and pear).

Bring to the boil and simmer (covered) on low heat for 1½ hours. If at any point the tagine looks dry, add a little extra stock or water, cover and continue to simmer until melt-in-the-mouth tender. Serve to baby warm with couscous or overcooked mushy rice.

IMPORTANT: remove the cinnamon stick before serving to baby.

Snuggly Chicken and Vermicelli Soup

Chicken soup – a home remedy used to soothe cold and flu symptoms for generations. So when Aaliyah had a cold, I felt compelled to rustle up some chicken soup to make her feel better. This soup contains cold- and flu-fighting Super Spices – cloves, cumin, cardamom and turmeric. It also includes immune-boosting vitamin A, selenium, and provides starch for energy. A tasty way to help replace lost fluids, soothe sore throats, and make your little one feel snuggly and warm inside.

1 tbsp olive oil
½ onion – peeled, chopped
2 whole cloves
1 whole cardamom pod – black
1 tsp minced garlic
1 chicken breast fillet
    (skinless) – cut into 1cm
    (½in) cubes
¼ tsp ground turmeric
Pinch of ground black pepper
½ tsp ground cumin
600ml (1 pint) hot chicken
    or vegetable stock –
    baby-friendly
1 medium carrot – washed,
    peeled, diced
80g (3oz) tinned sweetcorn
    (no added salt) – drained
25g (1oz) vermicelli

Heat the oil in a pot, add the onion, clove, and cardamom pod and stir-fry on medium-low heat for 3–4 mins until the onion is golden. Add the garlic and stir-fry for 30 secs–1 min, then add the chicken, turmeric, black pepper and cumin and cook for a further 5–8 mins.

Pour in the stock, add the carrot and sweetcorn, then over the pot, break the vermicelli into small pieces with your hands and toss in. Bring to the boil and simmer (uncovered) on medium-low heat for 6–8 mins until the veggies, chicken and vermicelli are tender.

Serve to baby warm on its own or with soft brown bread as a more filling meal.

IMPORTANT: remove the cloves and cardamom pod before serving to baby.

Mum's Lamb Curry with Sweet Potato

Lamb... my favourite red meat. When slow-cooked in curry, it absorbs all of the gorgeous aromatic spices and melts in the mouth. Lamb is an excellent source of essential amino acids (protein), omega 3 fatty acids, selenium, iron and zinc, which is necessary for good taste and smell senses. Combined with the benefits of beta-carotene (vitamin A) from the sweet potato, this is a wonderfully nutritious meal for baby.

2 tbsp olive oil
1 onion – peeled, chopped
2 whole cloves
1 small cinnamon stick
2 whole black peppercorns
1 whole cardamom pod – black
200g (7oz) lean lamb (boneless)
  – cut into 1cm (½in) cubes
½ tsp minced ginger
1 tsp minced garlic
¼ tsp ground turmeric
1 x 200g (7oz) tin chopped
  tomatoes
½ tsp ground cumin
½ tsp ground coriander
¼ tsp ground paprika
A squeeze of fresh lemon juice
  – ensuring no seeds fall in
350ml (12fl oz) water
1 tbsp plain unsweetened
  yogurt
1 small sweet potato –
  washed, peeled, cubed

Heat the oil in a pot, add the onion, cloves, cinnamon stick, peppercorns and cardamom pod and stir-fry on medium-low heat for 3–4 mins.

Then add the lamb, ginger, garlic and turmeric and stir-fry until the lamb is sealed. Add the tomatoes, cumin, coriander, paprika, lemon juice, water and yogurt. Bring to the boil and simmer (covered) for 1½ hours, or until the lamb is tender, stirring occasionally. If at any point the curry looks dry, add a little water.

While the curry is simmering, steam the sweet potato in either a steamer, or in the microwave by placing it in a microwavable dish and adding 2 tablespoons of water. Cover the dish with either a lid (leaving a small vent) or cling film (piercing a few holes), and steam on high for 4–5 mins until tender. Once cooked, drain off the excess water and add to the curry at the end. Combine well and serve to baby warm with roti or overcooked mushy rice.

IMPORTANT: remove the cloves, cinnamon stick, peppercorns and cardamom pod before serving to baby.

Family Super Meals

Stage 4 | 1–3 Years Plus

Congratulations! Now that your little one is a spice connoisseur, she has graduated on to Stage 4 – Family Super Meals! This is what we've been training her for!

There is no longer any need to cook separate family meals, so this chapter is about adapting your recipes and ensuring one meal is suitable for the whole family! And there is still no added salt, sugar or chillies in your little one's meals.

By this stage, when your baby is the tender age of one, you can also switch her over from breast milk or formula to whole cow's milk (full-fat), as a drink either in a cup or a free-flow beaker. As your little one will be getting most of her nutrients from food now, breast milk or formula is no longer necessary. That said, you can continue to breast feed your little one for as long as you both want to, so don't feel you need to give it up just yet.

Your little one should also be well on her way to enjoying three balanced meals and two or three healthy snacks per day. Happy days!

"When is the best time to introduce chillies?" I hear you ask… well, there is no strict rule about this. I would suggest introducing a mild chilli powder (just a pinch at a time), when you feel your little one is ready. This could be anywhere between 18 months to two years or later. When I was a child, I was eating the same heat as the rest of the family when I was just two! So it really depends on your little one's taste buds. Avoid fresh green chillies altogether until your little one is comfortable with red chilli powder, as fresh green chillies are extremely hot, hot, hot!

Toddler Eating Habits — What to Expect

Between the ages of 12–18 months, you'll notice your little one's motor skills will be further advanced, making her more independent, and so she'll be feeding herself with a spoon as well as using her hands. This newly found independence will also make her aware that she has a choice over what she eats, potentially causing mayhem at meal times.

In these situations, I found family meal times were great! Toddlers learn new behaviour by imitating what parents, siblings and peers do, so family meal times encouraged Aaliyah to eat nutritious meals, as she was eating the same food as the rest of the family. Setting her place at the dinner table was also great for making her feel recognised as a small 'grown-up' and an integral part of the family, which again encouraged her to eat her food.

Don't get me wrong, this was by no means the answer to every mother's eternal burning question... "How do I coax my little one into eating all of her food?" I still experienced difficult meal times whereby I desperately tried to persuade Aaliyah to eat her dinner, and she was more interested in decorating the floor with it. But it did play a role in reducing the amount of stressful mealtimes I experienced.

Another technique which encouraged Aaliyah to eat at mealtimes was involving her in our weekly shopping trips. As I'd wheel her around the supermarket in the shopping trolley, I'd ask her which fruit and vegetables we should buy. When she pointed out what she wanted, I allowed her to hold them for a while before she attempted to drop them on the floor, or whirl around and drop them behind her in the trolley. I found this worked really well for my little madam's independence, as she felt involved in the decision-making process.

Don't be alarmed if your little one appears to be eating less food. Within the first year, babies experience rapid growth, however, when they reach toddlerhood, their growth tends to slow down so the amount they eat will reflect this.

Also try not to get too stressed at meal times. It may appear that your little one has barely eaten one grain of rice, but toddlers will never let themselves go hungry. So switch off the TV and enjoy your family meals together. They are a time to eat healthy, tasty food, and to connect with the rest of the family, building precious moments that should be enjoyed and cherished for years to come.

> Tip: when eating a meal together, your little one may prefer to steal food from your plate rather than eat her own. In this situation put some of her food on your plate. When she tries to swipe your food, she will happily munch on her own thinking she is eating mummy or daddy's.

Aloo Gobi

White Super Foods are the main ingredients in this curry. Cauliflower (gobi), potatoes (aloo), ginger and garlic are all high in antioxidant activity. Cauliflower is high in vitamin C, which is great for healthy skin, brain function and immune system. The potatoes are a great source of potassium, essential for keeping our internal organs in good working condition.

2 tbsp olive oil
1 onion – peeled, chopped
1 tsp cumin seeds
1½ tsp minced garlic
1 tsp minced ginger
1 tsp ground coriander
½ tsp ground garam masala
¼ tsp ground turmeric
2 medium white potatoes –
   washed, peeled, cubed
200ml (7fl oz) water
400g (14oz) cauliflower florets
   – washed, chopped
Salt, to taste (optional)
Red chilli powder, to taste
   (optional)
Fresh coriander, for garnish –
   washed, chopped

Heat the oil in a large pot, add the onion and stir-fry until soft and golden. Add the cumin seeds, garlic, ginger, coriander, garam masala and turmeric and stir-fry for 30 secs–1 min to lightly cook the spices.

Add the potatoes and water and simmer (covered) on medium-low heat for 5 mins. Then add the cauliflower and an extra splash of water, cover and continue to simmer for 10–15 mins until both are tender.

Remove a serving for your little one and set aside. Then add salt and red chilli powder (if using) to the main pot and stir. Return to the heat for a further 1–2 mins to lightly cook the chilli.

Garnish the main servings (and your little one's) with fresh coriander and serve with roti or naan.

Bhindi Masala Curry

Bhindi (okra) is a popular vegetable in South Asian cuisine, however, if prepared incorrectly can be quite slimy and unpleasant in texture. The best method to avoid this slime is by lightly frying the bhindi before tossing it in with the curry sauce. Bhindi is rich in antioxidant vitamins A and C, is believed to be asthma preventative, and is good for digestion, too.

50ml (2fl oz) olive oil
400g (14oz) okra/bhindi – washed, chopped
1 onion – peeled, chopped
1½ tsp minced garlic
½ tsp ground cumin
½ tsp ground coriander
¼ tsp ground turmeric
1 tsp ground paprika
1 x 200g (7oz) tin chopped tomatoes
Juice of ½ lemon – ensuring no seeds fall in
Salt, to taste (optional)
Red chilli powder, to taste (optional)

Drizzle 1-2 tbsp of olive oil into a large, non-stick frying pan and lightly fry the bhindi on medium-low heat until they have browned slightly, and the slimy texture has gone. Remove from the pan, place on kitchen paper and set aside. Cook the bhindi in two batches, if necessary.

Using the same frying pan, add the 50ml (2fl oz) of oil and the onion to the pan and stir-fry on medium heat until the onions have browned. This will make a rich curry sauce.

Add the garlic, cumin, coriander, turmeric and paprika and stir-fry for a further 30 secs–1 min, then pour in the tomatoes and lemon juice. Simmer (uncovered) for 2–3 mins. Then add the bhindi to the masala, stir and simmer on low heat for a further 2–3 mins.

Once cooked, remove a serving for your little one and set aside. Add salt and red chilli powder (if using) to the main pot and stir. Return to the heat for a further 1–2 mins.

Serve with roti as a main dish, or alongside my Lamb Rogan Josh (page 162) as a side dish. Delicious!

Butternut Chickpea Curry

Chickpeas, members of the protein-rich food group, are an excellent source of fibre, folic acid and manganese – great for healthy skin. Combined with the Super Food health benefits of the butternut squash (beta-carotene), this is a sweet, tangy curry the whole family will reap the health rewards from!

50ml (2fl oz) olive oil
1 onion – peeled, chopped
2 tsp minced garlic
1 tsp ground cumin
¼ tsp ground turmeric
1 tsp ground paprika
1 tbsp tomato purée
¼ tsp ground black pepper
1 x 400g (14oz) tin chopped tomatoes
1 butternut squash – peeled, deseeded, cubed
250ml (8fl oz) water
1 x 400g (14oz) tin chickpeas – drained, washed
Salt, to taste (optional)
Ground cayenne pepper, to taste (optional)
Fresh coriander, for garnish – washed, chopped

Heat the oil in a large pot, add the onion and stir-fry on medium-low heat until soft and golden. Add the garlic and stir-fry for 30 secs–1 min, then add the cumin, turmeric, paprika, tomato purée and black pepper and stir-fry for another min to lightly cook the spices. Add the tomatoes and squash and pour in the water. Bring to the boil and simmer (covered) on a medium-low heat for 15 mins.

Then add the chickpeas, stir and simmer for a further 5 mins until the squash is tender. Once cooked, remove a serving for your little one and set aside.

Add salt and cayenne pepper (if using) to the main pot and stir. Return to the heat for a further 1–2 mins. Garnish the main servings (and your little one's) with fresh coriander and serve with couscous or rice.

Tip: tinned chickpeas are already cooked so there is no need to overcook them in the pot. Simply allow them to warm up and absorb the delicious flavours from the curry.

Tarka Coconut Dhal

This dhal requires the cooking technique 'tarka' or 'baghaar', whereby spices are intensely stir-fried in hot oil for a couple of minutes and poured over the dhal to give a strong burst of flavour. The dhal is also chock-full of healthy fats, fibre, protein and iron, and tastes extra yummy when eaten alongside my Masala Fish Curry (page 170). A match made in heaven!

Dhal:
2 tbsp olive oil
½ onion – peeled, chopped
1 tsp minced garlic
½ tomato – washed, deseeded, chopped
170g (6oz) red lentils – soaked in water (10 mins), washed, drained
250ml (8fl oz) unsweetened coconut milk
300ml (½ pint) water
¼ tsp ground turmeric
Salt, to taste (optional)
½ tsp red chilli powder (optional)

Tarka/Baghaar:
1 tbsp olive oil
1 tsp brown mustard seeds
½ onion – peeled, chopped
½ tomato – washed, deseeded, chopped
6–8 curry leaves
3–4 fresh green chillies – stems removed, washed, pounded to a paste

Dhal: Heat the oil in a large pot, add the onion, garlic and tomato and stir-fry on medium-low heat until the tomato is soft. Add the lentils, coconut milk, water and turmeric. Bring to the boil and simmer (uncovered) on medium-low heat for 15–20 mins until the lentils are tender. Once cooked, remove a serving for your little one and set aside. Add salt and the red chilli powder (if using) to the main pot and stir.

Tarka/Bhagaar: Just before serving, heat the oil in a frying pan, add the mustard seeds and stir-fry on medium-high heat until they begin to pop. Then add the onion, tomato and curry leaves. Continue to stir-fry for 2 mins, then add a teaspoon of the tarka (without curry leaves) to your little one's serving and combine well.

Add the green chillies to the remaining tarka and stir-fry for another min, before pouring over the main family dhal. Combine well and serve with rice or roti.

Matter Paneer

A South Asian vegetarian classic, comprising matter (peas) and paneer – a commonly used unsalted full-fat Indian cottage cheese. Once only available in specialist Indian grocers, it is now readily available at most supermarkets. Paneer is protein-rich and an excellent source of calcium, essential for building strong teeth and bones.

50ml (2fl oz) olive oil
225g (8oz) paneer – cubed
1 tsp cumin seeds
1 tsp minced garlic
3 tomatoes – washed, deseeded, chopped
¼ tsp ground turmeric
100ml (3½fl oz) water
1 tbsp tomato purée
225g (8oz) peas – frozen, washed
Salt, to taste (optional)
Red chilli powder, to taste (optional)

Drizzle 1-2 tbsp of olive oil into a large, non-stick frying pan and lightly fry the paneer on medium-low heat until the cubes turn golden. Remove from the pan, place on kitchen paper and set aside.

Using the same frying pan, add the 50ml (2fl oz) of oil, the cumin seeds and garlic to the pan and stir-fry on medium-low heat. When the seeds begin to splutter, add the tomatoes and stir-fry for 2–3 mins. Then add the turmeric, water and tomato purée and allow the sauce to simmer on medium heat for a few mins until it thickens.

Once cooked, add the paneer and peas, stir and simmer for 2–3 mins until the peas are tender, stirring occasionally.

Remove a serving for your little one and set aside. Then add salt and red chilli powder (if using) to the main pot and stir. Return to the heat for a further 1–2 mins to lightly cook the chilli. Serve with roti.

Simple Family Dhal

I love serving dhal (lentils) to my family. Good for the heart, high in iron and, due to its high-fibre nature, helps to regulate blood sugar levels by providing slow-burning energy. This family dhal is also quick and easy to prepare, and is a perfect accompaniment to any veggie or meat curry.

2 tbsp olive oil
1 onion – peeled, chopped
1 tsp brown mustard seeds
1 tomato – washed, deseeded, chopped
¼ tsp ground turmeric
1½ tsp cumin seeds
2 tsp minced garlic
1½ tsp minced ginger
170g (6oz) red lentils – soaked in water (10 mins), washed, drained
4 bay leaves
750ml (1¼ pints) water
Salt, to taste (optional)
Red chilli powder, to taste (optional)
Fresh coriander, for garnish – washed, chopped

Heat the oil in a large pot, add the onion and stir-fry until soft and golden. Add the mustard seeds, tomato, turmeric, cumin seeds, garlic and ginger and stir-fry for a further 2 mins. Add the lentils and bay leaves and pour in the water. Bring to the boil and simmer (covered) on medium-low heat for 15–20 mins until the lentils are tender.

Once cooked, remove a serving for your little one and set aside. Then add salt and red chilli powder to the main pot and stir. Return to the heat for a further 1–2 mins to lightly cook the chilli, although this isn't necessary. Garnish with fresh coriander and serve with roti or rice.

IMPORTANT: ensure there are no bay leaves included in baby's serving.

Big and Small Kofta Curry

The name of this kofta (meatball) curry was inspired by one of Aaliyah's favourite children's TV shows at the time, and for obvious reasons – big kofta are for adults and older children, smaller kofta are for toddlers. Make these kofta with whichever lean minced meat of your choice, either way they will be precious balls of protein-rich goodness.

Koftas:
500g (1lb 2oz) chicken/lamb mince
2 tsp minced garlic
1½ tsp ground garam masala
1 tsp ground cumin
½ tsp ground turmeric
4 fresh green chillies – stems removed, washed, pounded (optional)
1 tsp salt (optional)

Curry sauce:
75ml (3fl oz) olive oil
1 onion – peeled, chopped
2 (each) whole cloves, black peppercorns and cinnamon sticks
1 whole cardamom pod – black
½ tsp each minced ginger and garlic
¼ tsp ground turmeric
¾ tsp each ground cumin and coriander
1 tsp ground paprika
1 x 400g (14oz) tin chopped tomatoes
Salt, to taste (optional)
Red chilli powder, to taste (optional)
Fresh coriander, for garnish – washed, chopped

Kofta: In a bowl, place the mince, garlic and all the spices and combine well. Remove 100g (3½oz) serving for baby and roll into 1cm (½in) balls. Set aside. Add the green chillies and salt (if using) to the remaining mince and combine well. Roll into larger balls. Set aside.

Curry Sauce: Heat the oil in a large pot, add the onion, cloves, peppercorns, cinnamon sticks and cardamom pod and stir-fry on medium until the onions are browning. Add the ginger, garlic and remaining spices and stir-fry for a few secs, then add the tomatoes. Stir and cook the sauce for a few mins, then turn to low heat and add all the kofta balls gently. Simmer (covered) on low heat for 20–25 mins until the kofta are thoroughly cooked, stirring gently halfway through.

Once cooked, remove the small kofta balls, along with some sauce and set aside. Add salt and red chilli powder (if using) to the main pot and stir. Garnish with fresh coriander and serve with roti or naan and a dollop of plain yogurt.

IMPORTANT: ensure there are no whole spices included in baby's serving.

Cardamom Chicken Curry

Cooking a whole chicken (on the bone) gives this curry a unique flavour that cannot be replicated by using a chicken breast fillet. It really is scrumptious. Cardamom is the main Super Spice in this meal, providing a multitude of vitamins and minerals. Rich in vitamins A and C, potassium, iron and other B vitamins, cardamom is the little pod with big health benefits.

75ml (3fl oz) olive oil
6 whole cardamom pods –
   green, split
1 onion – peeled, chopped
1 tsp minced ginger
1½ tsp minced garlic
8–10 curry leaves
½ tsp ground turmeric
1 tsp ground coriander
¼ tsp ground black pepper
450g (1lb) tomatoes – washed,
   deseeded, chopped
1 tbsp tomato purée
150ml (¼ pint) water
1 whole chicken (skinless) –
   cut into 8 pieces, fat trimmed
3 fresh green chillies – stems
   removed, washed, pounded
   to a paste (optional)
Salt, to taste (optional)
Red chilli powder, to taste
   (optional)
Fresh coriander, for garnish –
   washed, chopped

Heat the oil in a large pot and add the cardamom pods, onion, ginger, garlic and curry leaves and stir-fry on medium heat until the onions are golden brown. Add the turmeric, coriander and black pepper and stir-fry for a few secs, then add the tomatoes, tomato purée and water. Simmer (uncovered) for 10 mins until the sauce becomes thick. Pop in the chicken pieces, add a little extra water if required, and simmer (covered) on low heat for 20–25 mins until the chicken is thoroughly cooked and tender and the sauce is creamy.

Remove a serving of 1–2 chicken pieces for your little one, including at least one piece of darker meat such as the leg, as darker meat contains more iron. Set aside. Add the green chillies, salt and red chilli powder (if using) to the main pot and stir. Return to the heat for a further 1–2 mins to lightly cook the chilli. Garnish the main serving (and your little one's) with fresh coriander and serve with roti, naan or rice.

IMPORTANT: ensure there are no cardamom pods, curry leaves or chicken bones included in baby's serving.

Indian Cottage Pie

Creamy, hearty, classic British pie with an Indian twist. Containing Worcestershire sauce, my initial thought was "there can't be any nutritional value in this condiment". But I was wrong! Worcestershire sauce is believed to boost immunity, build red blood cells and promote a healthy nervous system, as it's made using a mixture of ingredients rich in vitamin B6 (garlic, cloves and molasses).

Mash:
4 white potatoes – washed, peeled, cubed
150ml (¼ pint) whole milk
2 tbsp unsalted butter
¼ tsp ground black pepper

Pie Filling:
50ml (2fl oz) olive oil
1 onion – peeled, chopped
2 whole cardamom pods – black
2 tsp each minced garlic and ginger
2 tsp ground coriander
1½ tsp ground cumin
½ tsp ground black pepper
450g (1lb) lean beef mince
50ml (2fl oz) water
2 tbsp Worcestershire sauce
1 x 200g (7oz) tin chopped tomatoes
1 tbsp tomato purée
2 medium carrots – washed, peeled, diced
Salt, to taste (optional)
Ground cayenne pepper, to taste (optional)

Mash: Place the potatoes in a large pot, cover with water, bring to the boil and simmer (uncovered) until tender. Drain and mash. Then heat the milk and butter, add to the mashed potatoes along with the black pepper. Combine until smooth and creamy and set aside.

Pie filling: Heat the oil in a large frying pan, add the onion and cardamom pods and stir-fry until the onions are golden. Add the garlic, ginger and all the spices and stir-fry for 30 secs–1 min, then add the mince. Stir-fry until browned, then add the water, Worcestershire sauce, tomatoes, tomato purée and carrots, stir and bring to the boil. Simmer (covered) on medium-low heat for 15–20 mins, then remove the cardamom pods and leave to cool.

Preheat the oven to 180°C/350°F/gas mark 4. Remove a serving of mince for baby and place in a ramekin. Top with some of the mashed potatoes and set aside.

Add salt and cayenne pepper (if using) to the main pot, stir and spoon into a large ovenproof dish. Top with the remaining mashed potatoes. Place both dishes in the oven and bake for 30–35 mins. Cool slightly then serve with a side salad.

Indo-Moroccan Lamb Stew

A delectable iron- and protein-rich stew, enhanced by the gorgeous flavours and health benefits of the Super Spices: coriander, cinnamon, black pepper and garam masala. Containing antioxidant honey, this natural sweetener is anti-inflammatory, anti-viral and anti-bacterial, so it's excellent for treating cold and flu symptoms.

2 tbsp olive oil
1 onion – peeled, chopped
500g (1lb 2oz) lean lamb
   (boneless) – cubed
2 tsp minced garlic
600ml (1 pint) hot lamb or
   chicken stock – low salt
2 small cinnamon sticks
1 tsp clear runny honey
2 tsp ground garam masala
2 tsp ground coriander
½ tsp ground black pepper
80g (3oz) dried apricots –
   finely chopped
7g (¼oz) fresh mint leaves –
   washed, roughly chopped
25g (1oz) ground almonds

Heat the oil in a large pot, add the onion, lamb and garlic and stir-fry on medium heat until the lamb has browned. Add the stock, cinnamon sticks, honey, garam masala, coriander and black pepper and stir. Bring to the boil and simmer (covered) on low heat for 1 hour, stirring occasionally. Then add the apricots, half of the mint and the ground almonds to thicken the sauce. Continue to simmer (covered) for 30 mins until the lamb is melt-in-the-mouth tender.

Garnish the main serving (and your little one's) with the remaining mint and serve with couscous or rice.

Personally, I don't think this dish requires any extra salt, however, if you would like to add some, remove a serving for your little one before adding any to the main pot and stir.

Lamb Rogan Josh

Found on the menu of virtually every Indian restaurant, this curry is delicious and flavoursome. The green pepper adds some healthy greenery to this meal, making it rich in antioxidant vitamin C, lutein and zeaxanthin, as well as iron and protein.

75ml (3fl oz) olive oil
2 small cinnamon sticks
4 whole black peppercorns
4 whole cardamom pods – green, split
3 whole cloves
1 onion – peeled, chopped
2 tsp minced garlic
1½ tsp minced ginger
1 tsp cumin seeds
1 tsp ground coriander
2 tsp ground paprika
100ml (3½fl oz) plain unsweetened yogurt
450g (1lb) lean lamb (boneless) – cubed
350ml (12fl oz) water
1½ tbsp tomato purée
1 green pepper – washed, deseeded, diced
¼ tsp ground garam masala
Salt, to taste (optional)
Ground cayenne pepper, to taste (optional)
Fresh coriander, for garnish – washed, chopped

Heat the oil in a large pot and add the cinnamon sticks, peppercorns, cardamom pods and cloves. Stir-fry on medium-low heat until they sizzle, then add the onion and stir-fry until golden. Add the garlic, ginger, cumin seeds, coriander and paprika and stir-fry for a min.

Turn to low heat, add a splash of water and the yogurt, a little at a time, stirring continuously to avoid curdling. Then add the lamb and cook until the lamb is sealed.

Add the 350ml (12fl oz) water and tomato purée, stir and bring to the boil. Simmer (covered) on low heat for 1 hour 20 mins. Then pop in the green pepper, stir and continue to simmer (covered) for 8–10 mins until tender. Once cooked, remove a serving for your little one and set aside.

Sprinkle the garam masala and the salt and cayenne pepper (if using) over the main pot and stir. Garnish the main serving (and your little one's) with fresh coriander and serve with roti, rice or naan.

IMPORTANT: ensure there are no whole spices included in baby's serving.

Lamb, Saag and Aloo Curry

A scrummy curry containing the nutritional superhero spinach (saag)! This dark leafy green is rich in vitamin A (for a healthy immune system, skin and eyes), vitamin K (for healthy nervous system and strong bones), plus it is also anti-inflammatory, anti-cancer and rich in iron. Lamb is, however, the best source of iron and is also bursting with essential amino acids, necessary to keep our entire bodies in excellent working condition.

50ml (2fl oz) olive oil
1 onion – peeled, chopped
3 whole cloves
2 whole cardamom pods – black
4 whole black peppercorns
1 tsp cumin seeds
450g (1lb) lean lamb (boneless) – cubed
2 tsp minced garlic
1 tsp minced ginger
¼ tsp ground turmeric
1 x 400g (14oz) tin chopped tomatoes
250ml (8fl oz) water
1 tsp ground paprika
1½ tsp ground coriander
1 tbsp tomato purée
1 medium white potato – washed, peeled, cubed
300g (11oz) spinach leaves – washed thoroughly, chopped (no stems)
Salt, to taste (optional)
Red chilli powder, to taste (optional)

Heat the oil in a large pot and then layer the onion, cloves, cardamom pods, peppercorns and cumin seeds at the bottom, and top with the lamb, garlic, ginger and turmeric. Simmer (covered) on low heat for 10 mins. Add the tomatoes, water, paprika, coriander and tomato purée and stir. Bring to the boil and simmer (covered) on low heat for 1½ hours, stirring occasionally.

While the lamb is cooking, steam the potato in a steamer, or in the microwave with 2 tablespoons of water. Cover the dish with either a lid (leaving a small vent) or cling film (piercing a few holes), and steam on high for 3–4 mins or until tender. Drain and set aside. Next, steam the spinach for 2½ mins or until wilted using the same method, but DO NOT add any water. Drain and set aside.

Once the lamb is tender, add the cooked potato and spinach. Combine well, then remove a serving for your little one. Add salt and red chilli powder (if using) to the main pot and stir. Serve with naan, roti or rice.

IMPORTANT: ensure there are no whole spices included in baby's serving.

Mum's Chicken Karahi

My mum's chicken karahi is a favourite meal of mine. My mouth waters at the mere thought of eating it, yummy! So, needless to say it had to make an appearance in this book. The powerful antioxidant lycopene makes a double appearance in this curry from the chopped tomatoes and tomato purée, helping to keep cancer, heart disease and diabetes at bay.

75ml (3fl oz) olive oil
1 onion – peeled, chopped
2 tsp minced garlic
1½ tsp minced ginger
½ tsp ground turmeric
1 tsp ground cumin
1 tsp ground coriander
2 tsp ground paprika
300g (11oz) tinned
    chopped tomatoes
1 tbsp tomato purée
2 chicken breast fillets
    (skinless) – cubed
Salt, to taste (optional)
Red chilli powder, to taste
    (optional)
Fresh coriander, for garnish –
    washed, chopped

Heat the oil in a large pot, add the onion and stir-fry until soft and golden. Add the garlic and ginger and stir-fry for 30 secs–1 min, followed by the turmeric, cumin and coriander, paprika. Stir-fry for a few secs more, then add the tomatoes, tomato purée, stir and simmer (uncovered) on low heat until the sauce begins to thicken.

Add the chicken and simmer on medium-low heat for 10–15 mins until the chicken is cooked and tender, stirring occasionally.

Once cooked, remove a serving for your little one and set aside. Add salt and red chilli powder (if using) to the main pot and stir. Return to the heat for a further 1–2 mins to lightly cook the chilli.

Garnish the main serving (and your little one's) with fresh coriander and serve with rice or roti.

Tip: chicken breasts don't take long to cook, so keep an eye on this curry as overcooking the fillets can lead to tough meat.

Paprika Salmon Linguine

A super quick creamy pasta dish rich in vitamin A and calcium from the double cream. Although delicious, this is definitely one kept for special occasions due to the fat content of double cream. Nevertheless, the Super Food salmon provides a valuable source of vitamin D, high-quality protein and omega 3 fatty acids for the entire family.

400g (14oz) linguine
50ml (2fl oz) olive oil
1 onion – peeled, chopped
2 tsp minced garlic
1 tsp ground paprika
½ tsp ground nutmeg
¼ tsp ground black pepper
300ml (½ pint) double cream
4 x 125g (4oz) salmon fillets
　(skinless, boneless) – cubed
125g (4oz) peas – frozen,
　washed
Salt, to taste (optional)
Ground cayenne pepper,
　to taste (optional)
Fresh flat-leaf parsley for
　garnish – washed, chopped

Cook the linguine according to the packet instructions, then drain and set aside.

Meanwhile, heat the oil in a large pot, add the onion and stir-fry until golden. Add the garlic, paprika, nutmeg and black pepper and stir-fry for 30 secs and then pour in the double cream, add the salmon and simmer (covered) for 5–6 mins on low heat until the salmon chunks are flaky and break apart easily.

While the sauce is simmering, steam the peas in a steamer, or in the microwave with 2 tablespoons of water. Cover the dish with either a lid (leaving a small vent) or cling film (piercing a few holes), and steam on high for 1–1½ mins until tender. Once cooked, drain off the excess water and add to the sauce at the end. Combine well.

Remove a serving for your little one and set aside. Add salt and cayenne pepper (if using) to the main pot and stir. Return to the heat for 1–2 mins, then garnish both servings with parsley. Serve with the linguine.

IMPORTANT: ensure there are no fish bones included in baby's serving.

Masala Fish Curry

A gorgeous, tangy fish curry with a hint of fire (for the adults). For your little one, this is an excellent way to get some tasty fish into her diet. The lemon acts as a wonderful substitute for salt by providing a tart taste to the fish and, combined with the tomatoes, is a superb source of antioxidant vitamin C. The fish is also a great source of protein and B vitamins.

Marinade:
3 tbsp olive oil
1 tbsp tomato purée
1 tsp ground coriander
1 tsp ground cumin
1 tsp minced garlic
½ tsp ground turmeric
Juice of ½ lemon – freshly
   squeezed
Salt, to taste (optional)
4 x 100g (3½oz) white fish
   fillets (skinless, boneless)

Sauce:
3 tbsp olive oil
1 x 200g (7oz) tin chopped
   tomatoes
Salt, to taste (optional)
Red chilli powder, to taste
   (optional)
Fresh coriander, for garnish —
   washed, chopped

Marinade: Place the oil, tomato purée, coriander, cumin, garlic, turmeric and lemon juice in a bowl and combine. Remove 1 tablespoon of marinade and set aside – this will be used for the curry sauce later. Then cover 1 fish fillet (for baby) with the marinade and also set aside. Add salt (if using) to the remaining marinade and pour over the remaining fillets. Set aside for 30 mins.

Sauce: Heat the oil in a large frying pan, add the tomatoes and the reserved tablespoon of marinade. Simmer until the sauce thickens, then add the marinated fish fillets to the pan. Continue to simmer for 6–8 mins or until the fish is flaky. Turn over halfway through. Once cooked, remove baby's fish fillet and some curry sauce and set aside. Then add salt and red chilli powder (if using) to the pan and return to the heat for a further 1–2 mins. Garnish the main serving (and your little one's) with fresh coriander and serve with roti or rice, alongside my delicious Tarka Coconut Dhal (page 149).

IMPORTANT: ensure there are no fish bones included in baby's serving.

Quick Kids' Super Meals

These days Aaliyah is attending school, and when she comes home she's ravenous from all the concentrating and playing she's been doing. She needs some grub quickly to refuel, and I need to give her some food quickly to stop the grumbling. So my focus on her meals has shifted slightly. Nutrition is still my number one priority when it comes to her diet, but now I find myself looking for quick and easy snacks to feed her between meals.

So this chapter is about 'booster' snacks between meals that should take no longer than 15 minutes to prepare for your little one. They are simple, yummy, and are ALL still nutritional Super Meals!

I can honestly say I was always struggling for time, regardless of whether I was a stay-at-home mum looking after Aaliyah and trying to get the never-ending house work finished, or I was at work, coming home and still trying to get the never-ending house work finished! So with the lack of time being a major factor in people's lives, these recipes are perfect for whipping up healthy, nutritious meals or snacks in minutes.

I hope you find them useful. Absolute lifesavers for me!

Quick-cook Foods in Each Food Group

Carb-rich (starches)	Pasta	10–12 mins
	White basmati rice	10 mins
	Couscous	10 mins
	Roti/chapatti	ready-made, instant use
	Pitta	ready-made, instant use
	Bread (white and brown)	ready-made, instant use
Milk and Dairy	Cheese, milk, yogurt	ready-made, instant use
Protein-rich	Chicken breast fillet	10–15 mins
	Fish fillet	5–8 mins
	Eggs	3–5 mins
Vegetables	Various	between 2–10 mins to steam. Some take longer than others
Fruits	Various	many are ready for instant use – just require a little chopping time

Quick Meal Cooking Techniques

The Microwave is Your Friend: Speed up the cooking process by changing your cooking technique. For example, instead of boiling potatoes which can take 15 minutes (sometimes longer), steam them in the microwave for between 3–6 minutes depending on their size, and reduce cooking time by more than half. Alternatively, cook them using a steamer if you have one. Either way, both methods will help to maintain valuable nutrients in vegetables and will save you time.

Multi-task: Multi-tasking might be an obvious suggestion, but it's very easy to be so focussed on cooking one part of a meal, that you forget the other part. When I first started cooking, I'd concentrate on getting the curry right first, then after it was bubbling away, I'd put the rice on the hob to cook. It's only after I started cooking both at the same time (after I had Aaliyah), that multi-tasking saved me about 10–15 mins. This meant we were eating dinner earlier, which meant Aaliyah was getting ready for bed earlier, which in turn meant a little more relaxing time after she was in bed in the evenings.

Super Quick Bombay Potatoes

Bombay potatoes are a popular delicious snack or accompaniment to a larger family meal. Bursting with white Super Foods – garlic and potato – this snack is high in antioxidant activity. The potato is carb-rich, which is great for energy, and is also potassium-rich, necessary for healthy heart function. Mustard seeds are also antioxidant and rich in selenium, an anti-cancer mineral also found in chicken.

1 white potato – washed, peeled, cut into 2.5cm (1in) cubes
1½ tsp olive oil
¼ tsp brown mustard seeds
¼ tsp minced garlic
¼ tsp minced ginger
1 tbsp tomato purée

Place the potato cubes in a pot, cover with water, bring to the boil and simmer for 15 mins until tender. Drain and set aside.

Alternatively, save time and steam them in a steamer, or in the microwave by placing them in a microwavable dish and adding 2 tablespoons of water. Cover the dish with either a lid (leaving a small vent) or cling film (piercing a few holes), and steam on high for 3–4 mins until tender. Once cooked, drain and set aside.

While the potatoes are cooking, heat the oil in a non-stick frying pan on medium-low heat and add the mustard seeds. When they begin to sizzle and pop, turn to low heat and add the garlic and ginger and stir-fry for a few secs. Then immediately add a splash of water (be careful of the spits and sizzles) and the tomato purée and stir-fry until the tomato purée and water combine to form a masala sauce.

Finally, add the cooked potato cubes to the frying pan and combine with the masala. Cook for a further few secs, then remove from the heat. Serve warm.

Indian Salad Roti Wrap

I love Sambharo – a warm Indian salad, prepared using Super Foods cabbage and carrots, which are sautéed in a few spices and steamed until soft. And due to its uncomplicated nature, is a quick accompaniment to any Indian meal. This is a carb-rich snack (courtesy of the roti) which is great for providing kids with energy needed to play. Also rich in beta-carotene (carrots) and packed with white antioxidant Super Foods (garlic and cabbage), I would highly recommend including this simple, delicious snack regularly in a child's diet.

Sambharo:
1 tbsp olive oil
1½ tsp brown mustard seeds
2 tsp minced garlic
½ white cabbage – washed, finely chopped
4 medium carrots – washed, peeled, grated (using a food processor)
1 tsp ground turmeric

To serve (one serving):
1 roti – homemade or ready-made, warmed
2–3 tbsp sambharo – warm
Dollop of Greek-style plain yogurt
Fresh coriander, for garnish – washed, chopped

Sambharo: Heat the oil in a frying pan on medium-low heat, add the mustard seeds and garlic and stir-fry until the seeds begin to pop and sizzle. Then add the cabbage and carrots and sprinkle over the turmeric. Stir to combine well, then leave to steam (covered) on low heat until the cabbage is soft; this will take between 5–7 mins.

To serve (one serving): Place a warm roti on a plate, spoon the sambharo in a line down the centre of the roti. Drizzle over some Greek-style yogurt and top with fresh coriander. Roll and cut in half for easy eating.

Repeat as necessary for up to four kids, and enjoy!

Tip: if you choose to cook cabbage for any other meal, the best way to preserve the nutrients is by sautéing the cabbage.

Baked Bean Curry

Now this fabulous curry is as quick to make as it is to warm up the tin of beans it comes from! Perfect served as lunch for a 3–4-year-old or as an after-school snack for older children. Baked beans are low in fat and are protein- and fibre-rich, plus provide other important minerals – iron, folic acid, zinc and potassium.

1½ tsp olive oil
½ tsp minced garlic
½ tsp brown mustard seeds
½ tsp cumin seeds
1 x 200g (7oz) tin baked beans
  – low-salt/low-sugar variety
Pinch of ground ginger
¼ tsp ground coriander
Pinch of ground turmeric
Pinch of ground black pepper

Heat the oil in a small pot on low heat and add the garlic, mustard seeds and cumin seeds. Stir-fry for 2 mins allowing the seeds to sizzle for a little while, then add the baked beans and stir.

Add the ginger, coriander, turmeric and black pepper, stir and then simmer for 5 mins on low heat and it's done! Remove from the heat and set aside.

Serve alongside some warm buttery granary toast for my twist on the British classic – beans on toast. Alternatively, serve with a baked potato for a more filling meal.

Tip: Creating two servings from this curry reduces the salt content by half and keeps your child's salt intake low.

Mini Masala Omelettes

I like to call these little gems protein-rich pancakes! Excellent for healthy growth, as well as being delicious, and the teeny weeny size makes them very appealing to kids. Add a few aromatic spices for extra flavour and this one will become a firm after-school favourite.

1 egg
¼ small onion – peeled, finely chopped
2 baby plum tomatoes (or ¼ regular tomato) – washed, deseeded, chopped
Pinch of ground black pepper
Pinch of ground garam masala
Pinch of ground cumin
3–4 fresh coriander leaves – washed, finely chopped
Salt, to taste (optional)
1 tsp olive oil

Crack the egg into a bowl and add the onion, tomatoes, black pepper, garam masala, cumin, coriander leaves and salt (if using), and whisk the whole lot together.

Pour the oil into a small, non-stick frying pan, heat the oil, then add half of the egg mixture. Cook on medium-low heat for a few mins until the top is no longer runny, then turn it over and cook on the other side for another min or two. Remove from the pan and repeat for the second omelette. Serve with roti or with warm buttered toast and a side of salad.

Tip: if you don't have a small frying pan to make mini omelettes, make one larger one instead.

Fragrant Sweet Pepper Pilaf

The fragrance in this snack comes from gorgeous whole spices the rice is cooked with – cinnamon, cloves and cardamom. Extremely quick to cook, this is a hassle-free one-pot meal that provides your little one with an extra little energy boost before dinner.

50ml (2fl oz) olive oil
1 onion – peeled, chopped
1½ tsp minced garlic
1 cinnamon stick
2 whole cloves
2 cardamom pods – green
200g (7oz) white basmati rice
375ml (13fl oz) water
Salt, to taste
1 red or yellow pepper –
　washed, deseeded, diced

Heat the oil in a pot, add the onion, cinnamon stick, cloves and cardamom pods. Stir-fry until the onion is soft and golden. Add the garlic, stir-fry for a min, then add the rice, water and salt and stir. Bring to the boil and simmer (covered) for 10 mins until the rice is tender. Switch off the heat and allow the rice to continue to steam for a further 2–3 mins (covered).

Once finished, fluff up the rice with a fork, add the pepper for a sweet crunch, combine well with the rice and serve with a side salad.

Tip: serve this rice as an accompaniment to evening meals for a twist on your everyday rice.

IMPORTANT: ensure all whole spices are removed from the pot before serving.

APPENDIX I – *Food Storage Guidelines*

Food type	Preparation	Freezing	Refrigerating	Heating
Curries	Cook 2–3 different curries at a time – one protein/one veggie to ensure a balanced diet. Allow to cool and prepare individual servings (see appendix II).	Ensure your freezer is set to 0°F (-18°C) or below, and curries will keep for 6–8 weeks.	Store in the fridge for up to 48 hours.	From frozen – thaw in the fridge/microwave. Heat until piping hot, then allow to cool before serving. From chilled – heat until piping hot, then allow to cool before serving. Important: ALWAYS test the temperature to ensure there are no hotspots.
Pitta bread (ready-made)	N/A	Freeze on day of purchase. Will keep for 6–8 weeks.	Once packet opened, will last for up to 72 hours, sometimes longer.	From frozen – thaw in the fridge, microwave or toaster. Heat until piping hot, then allow to cool before serving. From chilled – heat in the microwave, oven, grill or toaster. Allow to cool before serving.
Quinoa	Allow cooked quinoa to cool and prepare immediately into individual servings (see appendix II)	Ensure your freezer is set to 0°F (-18°C) or below, and quinoa will keep for 6–8 weeks.	Store in the fridge for up to 48 hours.	From frozen – thaw in the fridge/microwave. Heat until piping hot, then allow to cool before serving. From chilled – heat until piping hot, then allow to cool before serving. Important: ALWAYS test the temperature to ensure there are no hotspots.
Rice	Lay freshly cooked rice flat on a tray and allow to cool, then prepare individual servings (see appendix II), and immediately place in the fridge/freezer to avoid bacterial growth when the rice is at room temperature.	Ensure your freezer is set to 0°F (-18°C) or below, and rice will keep for 6–8 weeks.	Store in the fridge for up to 48 hours.	From frozen – thaw in the fridge/microwave. Heat until piping hot, then allow to cool before serving. From chilled – heat until piping hot, then allow to cool before serving. Important: ALWAYS test the temperature to ensure there are no hotspots.
Roti (home-made)	Lay freshly cooked rotis flat on the counter or on a tray and allow to cool. Then collect in a pile, wrap in foil and place in a large freezer bag and seal.	Ensure your freezer is set to 0°F (-18°C) or below, and one batch of rotis will keep for 6–8 weeks. Note: one frozen roti pulls apart from the batch easily.	One batch will last for up to 72 hours, sometimes longer.	From frozen – thaw in the fridge/microwave. Heat until piping hot, then allow to cool before serving. From chilled – heat until piping hot, then allow to cool before serving.
Roti (ready-made)	N/A	Freeze on day of purchase. Will keep for 6–8 weeks.	Once packet opened, will last for up to 72 hours, sometimes longer.	From frozen – thaw in the fridge/microwave. Heat until piping hot, then allow to cool before serving. From chilled – heat until piping hot, then allow to cool before serving.

APPENDIX II – *Individual Serving Sizes*

Stages	Individual Serving Sizes
Stage 2 | 7 Months Plus	1 serving = 2 tablespoons
Stage 3 | 10 Months Plus	1 serving = 3 tablespoons

You may need to increase or reduce the amount, depending on your little one's appetite.

Storage Advice

Store individual servings in good quality freezer bags, label them with the contents, date them and place them in the freezer. A flawless way of effectively rotating frozen freshly cooked food. Furthermore, freezer bags are handy for squeezing into corners if you are tight for space.

Alternatively, freeze baby food in flexible ice-cube trays, but ensure the tray is covered with either a lid or placed inside a freezer bag, before it is placed in the freezer; it must be clearly labelled with the contents. Once frozen, remove the baby food cubes from the tray, place them in freezer bags, label and date them, then pop them back in the freezer.

APPENDIX III – *Cooking Conversion Tables and Abbreviations*

Abbreviations

fl oz	fluid ounce
g	gram
lb	pound
ml	millilitre
oz	ounce
tbsp	tablespoon
tsp	teaspoon

Spoon Conversions

1 x UK teaspoon	5ml
1 x UK tablespoon	15ml (3 teaspoons)

Liquid Conversions

Metric	Imperial	Cups
50ml	2fl oz	¼ cup
125ml	4fl oz	½ cup
175ml	6fl oz	¾ cup
250ml	8fl oz	1 cup

Please note: all conversions are approximate.

Index

Resources, References and Links

Articles

Ahuja, P. 2009. **Health Benefits of Nutmeg.** Complete Wellbeing. [ONLINE] 16 August. Available at: http://completewellbeing. com/article/a-nutty-affair/ [Accessed 14 March 2012]

Associated Newspapers Ltd. 2005. **The Top 10 Super foods.** Mail Online, [ONLINE] (Last updated at 10:55 22 December 2005). Available at: http://www.dailymail.co.uk/ health/article-369042/The-10-super-foods.html [Accessed 8 February 2012]

Associated Press. 2005. **Experts Seek to Debunk Baby Food Myths.** msnbc.com, [ONLINE] (Last updated 10.45 PM on 09th October 2005). Available at: http://www. msnbc.msn.com/id/9646449/#. TzDvmVyRFhwU [Accessed 20 September 2011]

Bennett, Coleman and Co. 2012. **Use Herbs, Spices to Keep Cold at Bay.** The Times of India, [ONLINE] 9 January. Available at: http://articles.timesofindia.indiatimes. com/2012-01-09/kanpur/30607134_1_ indian-spice-winter-ailments-cloves [Accessed 11 January 2012]

Bond, AB. 2005. **Top 12 Super Food Herbs and Spices.** Care2, [ONLINE] 30 March. Available at: http://www.care2.com/ greenliving/top-12-Super Food-herbs-and-spice.html#ixzz1jStivjXK [Accessed 18 January 2012]

Cespedes, A. 2010. **Worcestershire Sauce Nutrition.** Livestrong.com, [ONLINE] 31 December. Available at: http://www. livestrong.com/article/346527-worcestershire-sauce-nutrition/ [Accessed 17 April 2012]

Ericson, J. 2014. **Oregano Oil Fights Norovirus: Carvacrol Shown to Kill Foodborne Pathogen, Hints At New Disinfectant.** Medical Daily. [ONLINE] 11 February. Available at: http://www. medicaldaily.com/oregano-oil-fights-norovirus-carvacrol-shown-kill-foodborne-pathogen-hints-new-disinfectant-269123 [Accessed 17 March 2014]

Evans, K. 2011. **Flavonoids in Fruits, Vegetables and Nuts Dramatically Lower Cancer Rates.** Natural News.com, [ONLINE] 28 September. Available at: http://www. naturalnews.com/033708_cancer_ flavonoids.html [Accessed 7 December 2011]

Gasior, K. 2011. **The Benefits of Paprika.** Livestrong.com [ONLINE] (Last updated on 8th September 2011). Available at: http:// www.livestrong.com/article/539058-the-benefits-of-paprika/ [Accessed 31 March 2012]

Hari, S, M.D. 1995. **Free Radicals: A Major Cause of Aging and Disease.** Consumer Health, [ONLINE] Available at: http://www. consumerhealth.org/articles/display. cfm?ID=19990303172533 [Accessed 8 March 2012]

Jockers, D, Dr. 2010. **Discover the Super Food power of coconut.** Natural News.com [ONLINE] 25 September. Available at: http://www.naturalnews.com/029841_ coconut_Super Food.html [Accessed 19 October 2011]

Kassem, N. 2011. **Nutritional content of Honey.** Livestrong.com [ONLINE] 10 February. Available at: http://www. livestrong.com/article/378810-nutritional-content-of-honey/ [Accessed 30 April 2012]

Keefer, A. 2011. **Calcium Absorption and Potassium.** Livestrong.com [ONLINE] 1 September. Available at: http://www. livestrong.com/article/528043-calcium-absorption-potassium/ [Accessed 19 December 2011]

Kellow, J, BSc RD. 2000. **From Snack Foods to Super Foods – Pop Corn and Whole Grain Cereals.** Weight Loss Resources, [ONLINE] Available at: http://www. weightlossresources.co.uk/food/healthy/ Super Foods/pop-corn-whole-grain-breakfast-cereals.htm [Accessed 22 March 2012]

Kovacs, B, MS, RD. 2012. **Probiotics.** MedicineNet.com [ONLINE] Available at: http://www.medicinenet.com/probiotics/article.htm [Accessed 7 March 2012]

Laurance, J. 2007. **The Big Question. What Are Super Foods and Are They Really So Good For Our Health?** The Independent, [ONLINE] 16 February. Available at: http:// www.independent.co.uk/life-style/ health-and-families/health-news/the-big-question-what-are-Super Foods-and-are-they-really-so-good-for-our-health-436529. html [Accessed 3 February 2012]

Magee, E, MPH, RD. 2007. **The Super-Veggies: Cruciferous Vegetables.** WebMD, [ONLINE] 19 April. Available at: http:// www.webmd.com/food-recipes/features/ super-veggies-cruciferous-vegetables [Accessed 6 March 12]

Maternowski, T. 2011. **Does Eating Pepper Affect the Unborn Baby?** Livestrong.com, [ONLINE] 28 March. Available at:http:// www.livestrong.com/article/258605-does-eating-pepper-affect-the-unborn-baby/ [Accessed 12 October 2011]

MedicalDaily.com. 2010. **Health Benefits of Mangoes.** Medical Daily [ONLINE] 7 November. Available at: http://www. medicaldaily.com/news/20101107/3414/ health-benefits-of-mangoes.htm [Accessed 14 March 2012]

MediLexicon International Ltd. 2009. **Common Food Allergies.** Medical News Today, [ONLINE] 12 May. Available at: http://www. medicalnewstoday.com/releases/8624.php [Accessed 16 September 2011]

MediLexicon International Ltd. 2009. **Oleocanthal May Help Prevent/Treat Alzheimer's.** Medical News Today, [ONLINE] 30 September. Available at: http://www. medicalnewstoday.com/releases/165611. php [Accessed 9 February 2012]

MediLexicon International Ltd. 2004. **What are Proteins?** Medical News Today, [ONLINE] 23 September. Available at: http://www.medicalnewstoday.com/ releases/13903.php [Accessed 26 January 2012]

Nakauchi, L. 2011. **Lady Finger Herb Provides Colon Health.** Natural News.com [ONLINE] 8 October. Available at: http://www. naturalnews.com/033807_colon_health_ lady_finger.html [Accessed 2 May 2012]

Phillip, J. 2011. **Black Raspberries and Anthocyanin's Demonstrate Powerful Cancer Fighting Power.** Natural News.com [ONLINE] 14 April. Available at: http:// www.naturalnews.com/032068_black_ raspberries_cancer.html [Accessed 16 February 2012]

Roberts, M. 2012. **Spoon Feeding 'Makes Babies Fatter'.** BBC News Health, [ONLINE] (Last updated 01:48 on 7th February 2012). Available at: http://www.bbc.co.uk/news/ health-16905371 [Accessed 10 February 2012]

Sample, I. 2008. **Health: Breastfed Babies More Receptive to Tastes, Say Food Research Scientists.** The Guardian,

[ONLINE] 24 July. Available at: http://www.guardian.co.uk/science/2008/jul/24/humanbehaviour.foodtech [Accessed 30 September 2011]

ScienceDaily LLC. 2005. **Raisins As A Functional Food for Oral Health.** ScienceDaily, [ONLINE] 13 June. Available at: http://www.sciencedaily.com/releases/2005/06/050613062724.htm [Accessed 13 March 2012]

Selke, LA. 2010. **What Kind of Spices Can I Use in My Baby's Food?** Livestrong.com, [ONLINE] 2 September. Available at: http://www.livestrong.com/article/218627-what-kind-of-spices-can-i-use-in-my-babys-food/ [Accessed 17 September 2011]

Telegraph Media Group Ltd. 2011. **Health benefits of Vitamin D.** The Telegraph. [ONLINE] 12 April. Available at: http://www.telegraph.co.uk/health/healthnews/8444739/Health-benefits-of-vitamin-D.html [Accessed 12 October 2011]

Uher, P. 2010. **Health Benefits of Cardamom.** Helium, [ONLINE] 4 March. Available at: http://www.helium.com/items/1761448-what-are-the-health-benefits-of-the-spice-cardamom [Accessed 21 March 2012]

University of Maryland Medical Center. 2011. **Manganese.** [ONLINE] (Last updated on 10th July 2011). Available at: http://www.umm.edu/altmed/articles/manganese-000314.htm [Accessed 31 January 2012]

University of Maryland Medical Center. 2011. **Omega-3 fatty acids.** [ONLINE] (Last updated on 10th May 2011). Available at: http://www.umm.edu/altmed/articles/omega-3-000316.htm [Accessed 7 March 2012]

Vandermark, T. 2011. **The Nutritional Benefits of Eggplant.** Livestrong.com, [ONLINE] (Last updated on 26th April 2011). Available at: http://www.livestrong.com/article/19046-nutritional-benefits-eggplant/ [Accessed 28 September 2011]

Vandermark, T. 2011. **What Is the Nutritional Value of Dates?** Livestrong.com, [ONLINE] (Last updated on 26th April 2011. Available at: http://www.livestrong.com/article/17923-nutritional-value-dates/ [Accessed 13 March 2012]

Walling, E. 2009. **Learn About the Many Benefits of Lauric Acid in Coconut oil.** Natural News.com [ONLINE] 11 August. Available at: http://www.naturalnews.com/026819_lauric_acid_coconut_oil_infections.html [Accessed 19 October 2011]

Zelman, K, MPH, RD/LD. 2008. **The Benefits of Vitamin C.** MedicineNet.com, [ONLINE] 4 April. Available at: http://www.medicinenet.com/script/main/art.asp?articlekey=88519 [Accessed 6 March 2012]

Books and Journals

Chaturvedi TP. 2009. **Uses of Turmeric in Dentistry: An Update.** Indian J Dent Res. [E-JOURNAL] 20 (1): 107-109. Available at: http://www.ijdr.in/text.asp?2009/20/1/107/49065 [Accessed 4 October 2011]

Department of Health. 2009. **NHS Birth to Five.** London: Produced by COI

Dewanto, V, Wu, X and Liu, RH. 2002. **Processed Sweet Corn has Higher Antioxidant Activity.** J. Agric. Food Chem. [E-JOURNAL] 50 (17) 4959 −4964. Abstract only. Available at: http://pubs.acs.org/doi/abs/10.1021/jf0255937 [Accessed 10 February 2012]

Jagetia GC and Aggarwal BB. 2007. "Spicing Up" of the Immune System by Curcumin. J Clin Immunol. [E-JOURNAL] 27 (1): 19-35. Available at: http://www.curcuminresearch.org/PDF/Jagetia%20GC-21.pdf [Accessed 2 October 2011]

Karmel, A. 2001. Annabel Karmel's Super Foods for Babies and Children. London: Ebury Press.

Mennella JA, PhD, Jagnow CP and Beauchamp GK, PhD. (2001) Prenatal and Postnatal Flavor Learning by Human Infants. Pediatrics. [E-JOURNAL] 107 (6): E88. Available at: http://www.ncbi.nlm.nih.gov/pmc/articles/PMC1351272/pdf/nihms-5608.pdf [Accessed 28 September 2011]

Rajeshwari U and Andallu B. 2011. Medicinal Benefits of Coriander (Coriandrum Sativum L).Spatula DD. [E-JOURNAL] 1 (1), 51-58. Available at: http://www.scopemed.org/fulltextpdf.php?mno=2633 [Accessed 26 October 2011]

Shobana, K and Naidu, A. 2000. Antioxidant Activity of Selected Indian Spices. PLEFA. [E-JOURNAL] 62 (2), 107-110. Abstract only. Available at: http://www.sciencedirect.com/science/article/pii/S095232789990128X [Accessed 7 November 2011]

Skulas-Ray et al. 2011. A High Antioxidant Spice Blend Attenuates Postprandial Insulin and Triglyceride Responses and Increases Some Plasma Measures of Antioxidant Activity in Healthy, Overweight Men. J Nutr. [E-JOURNAL] 10, 3945. 1-7. Available at: http://jn.nutrition.org/content/early/2011/06/22/jn.111.138966.full.pdf [Accessed 10 January 2012]

Sommerburg O, Keunen JEE, Bird AC and Van Kuijk FJGM. 1998. Fruits and Vegetables That Are Sources for Lutein and Zeaxanthin: The Macular Pigment in Human Eyes. Br J Ophthalmol. [E-JOURNAL] 82, 907-910. Available at: http://www.ncbi.nlm.nih.gov/pmc/articles/PMC1722697/pdf/v082p00907.pdf [Accessed 7 December 2011]

Fact Sheets

Condé Nast. 2012. Self-Nutrition Data – Cream, Fluid, Heavy Whipping. [ONLINE] Available at: http://nutritiondata.self.com/facts/dairy-and-egg-products/51/2 [Accessed 8 May 2012]

Department of Health. 2011. NHS Introducing Solid Foods. Giving Your Baby a Better Start in Life. [PDF] Available at: http://www.dh.gov.uk/prod_consum_dh/groups/dh_digitalassets/documents/digitalasset/dh_125828.pdf [Accessed 22 November 2011]

Food – a fact of life. 2009. Estimated Average Requirements (EARS) for Energy. [ONLINE] Available at: http://www.google.co.uk/url?sa=tandrct=jandq=andesrc=sandsource=webandcd=1andsqi=2andved=0CFQQFjAAandurl=http%3A%2F%2Fwww.foodafactoflife.org uk%2Fattachments%2Fbffoc546-9cf1-485db51d1cf2.docandei=K8D2T82tNumYoQXniKilBwandusg=AFQjCNErLbXck47XLYYuWYlw_1uI-ujBBA [Accessed 6 March 2012]

Nutrition-and-you.com. 2010. Cardamom Nutrition Facts. [ONLINE] – Available at: http://www.nutrition-and-you.com/cardamom.html [Accessed 5 March 2012]

Office of Dietary Supplements – National Institutes of Health. 2009. Folate. [ONLINE] (Last reviewed on 15th April 2009). Available at: http://ods.od.nih.gov/factsheets/folate/ [Accessed 7 March 2012]

Office of Dietary Supplements – National Institutes of Health. 2011. **Selenium.** [ONLINE] (Last reviewed 11th October 2011). Available at: http://ods.od.nih.gov/factsheets/Selenium-HealthProfessional/ [Accessed 20 February 2012]

Office of Dietary Supplements – National Institutes of Health. 2011. **Zinc.** [ONLINE] (Last reviewed on 20th September 2011). Available at: http://ods.od.nih.gov/factsheets/Zinc-HealthProfessional/ [Accessed 24 February 2012]

Reports

Food Standards Agency. 2001. **Expert Group on Vitamins and Minerals – Revised Review of Vitamin C.** [ONLINE] Available at: http://www.food.gov.uk/multimedia/pdfs/vitaminc.pdf [Accessed 5 January 2012]

Health & Social Care Information Centre. 2013. **National Child Measurement Programme: England, 2012/13 School Year.** [ONLINE] Available at: http://www.hscic.gov.uk/catalogue/PUB13115/nati-chil-meas-prog-eng-2012-2013-rep.pdf [Accessed 1 January 2014]

U.S. Department of Agriculture. 2009. **National Nutrient Database for Standard Reference, Release 22. Lycopene (μg) Content of Selected Foods per Common Measure, sorted by nutrient content.** [ONLINE] Available at: http://www.ars.usda.gov/SP2UserFiles/Place/12354500/Data/SR22/nutrlist/sr22w337.pdf [Accessed 9 December 2011]

U.S. Department of Agriculture. 2010. **USDA Database for the Oxygen Radical Absorbance Capacity (ORAC) of Selected Foods, Release 2.** [ONLINE] Available at: http://www.orac-info-portal.de/download/ORAC_R2.pdf [Accessed 18 October 2011]

Websites

American Cancer Society. 2008. **Ellagic Acid. Find Support and Treatment.** [ONLINE] (Last updated on 1st November 2008). Available at: http://www.cancer.org/Treatment/TreatmentsandSideEffects/ComplementaryandAlternativeMedicine/DietandNutrition/ellagic-acid [Accessed 6 February 2012]

American Cancer Society. 2010. **Lycopene. Find Support and Treatment.** [ONLINE] (Last updated on 13th May 2011). Available at: http://www.cancer.org/Treatment/TreatmentsandSideEffects/ComplementaryandAlternativeMedicine/DietandNutrition/lycopene [Accessed 6 February 2012]

AntioxidantsDetective.com. 2009. **The Benefits of Selenium.** [ONLINE] Available at: http://www.antioxidantsdetective.com/benefits-of-selenium.html [Accessed 15 February 2012]

Antioxidants-for-Health-and-Longevity.com. 2009. **Cumin Health Benefits Come from Antioxidants.** [ONLINE] Available at: http://www.antioxidants-for-health-and-longevity.com/cumin-health-benefits.html [Accessed 11 January 2012]

Antioxidants-for-health-and-longevity.com. 2009. **Health Benefits of Cloves Nature's Top Antioxidant Food.** [ONLINE] Available at: http://www.antioxidants-for-health-and-longevity.com/benefits-of-cloves.html [Accessed 11 January 2012]

Baby Center India. 2008. **When And How Should I Add Spices in My Baby's Food?** [ONLINE] Available at: http://www.babycenter.in/baby/startingsolids/spicesinbabyfoodexpert/ [Accessed 17 September 2011]

Baby Centre. 2009. **Food Allergies.** [ONLINE] Available at: http://www.babycentre.co.

uk/baby/startingsolids/foodallergies/ [Accessed 18 August 2011]

BBC Health. 2012. **Weaning.** [ONLINE] Available at: http://www.bbc.co.uk/health/physical_ health/child_development/babies_ weaning.shtml [Accessed 2 January 2012]

Christine. 2009. **The Goodness of Garlic for Baby.** Home Made Baby Food Recipes Blog [BLOG] 6 November. Available at: http:// blog.homemade-baby-food-recipes.com/ the-goodness-of-garlic-for-baby/ [Accessed 19 September 2011]

Christine. 2009. **Why Turmeric Is One of The Best Spices You Can Give Your Baby.** Home Made Baby Food Recipes Blog [BLOG] 10 September. Available at: http:// blog.homemade-baby-food-recipes.com/ why-turmeric-is-one-of-the-best-spices- you-can-give-your-baby/ [Accessed 19 September 2011]

Coconut Research Centre. 2004. **Coconut.** [ONLINE] Available at: http://www. coconutresearchcenter.org/ [Accessed 19 October 2011]

Condon, S. 1997. **Is It Okay to Eat Spicy Food While Nursing?** Baby Centre [ONLINE] Available at: http://wwww.babycenter. com/404_is-it-okay-to-eat-spicy-food- while-nursing_1931.bc [Accessed 6 September 2011]

Garden-Robinson, J, Ph.D., L.R.D. 2011. **What Color is Your food? Taste a Rainbow of Fruit and Vegetables for Better Health.** North Dakota State University [ONLINE] (Last reviewed May 2011). Available at: http://www.ag.ndsu.edu/pubs/yf/foods/ fn595w.htm [Accessed 5 February 2012]

Healthaliciousness.com. 2008. **Top 10 Foods Highest in Beta Carotene.** [ONLINE] Available at: http://www. healthaliciousness.com/articles/

natural-food-sources-of-beta-carotene. php [Accessed 29 February 2012]

Healthaliciousness.com. 2008. **Top 10 Foods Highest in Lycopene.** [ONLINE] Available at: http://www.healthaliciousness.com/ articles/high-lycopene-foods.php. [Accessed 29 February 2012]

Healthaliciousness.com. 2008. **Top 10 Foods Highest in Vitamin A.** [ONLINE] Available at: http://www. healthaliciousness.com/articles/ food-sources-of-vitamin-A.php[Accessed 29 February 2012]

Health Diaries. 2010. **Eat This! – 6 Health Benefits of Lentils.** [ONLINE] 7 November. Available at: http://www.healthdiaries. com/eatthis/6-health-benefits-of-lentils. html [Accessed 20 December 2011]

Homemade Baby Food Recipes. 2011. **Can Babies Eat Spicy Food?** [ONLINE] (Last updated on 1st June 2011). Available at: http://www.homemade-baby-food- recipes.com/can-babies-eat-spicy-food. html [Accessed 19 September 2011]

Home Remedies Web.com. 2006. **Cinnamon Health Benefits.** [ONLINE] Available at: http://www.homeremediesweb.com/ cinnamon_health_benefits.php [Accessed 11 November 2011]

Hood, KJM. 2011. **Paneer Cheese and Its Health Benefits!** Sjogren's Syndrome Blog. [ONLINE] 12 October. Available at: http://sjogrensblog.org/2011/10/12/ paneer-cheese-and-its-health-benefits/ [Accessed 26 April 2012]

Lovinelli, BM, RN, BSN, IBCLC. 2011. **When Can Babies Have Spices in Their Food?** Baby Zone [ONLINE] Available at: http:// www.babyzone.com/askanexpert/ baby-spices-solid-food [Accessed 19 September 2011]

Lycopene benefits.org. 2012. **Lycopene benefits.**[ONLINE] Available at: http://lycopenebenefits.org/ [Accessed 6 February 2012]

McCormick Science Institute. 2009. **Spices, Herbs and Antioxidants.** [ONLINE] Available at: http://www.mccormickscienceinstitute.com/content.cfm?ID=10437 [Accessed 22 October 2011]

MedlinePlus. 2011. **B Vitamins.** [ONLINE] Available at: http://www.nlm.nih.gov/medlineplus/bvitamins.html [Accessed 6 March 2012]

MedlinePlus. 2010. **Potassium in Diet.** [ONLINE] Available at: http://www.nlm.nih.gov/medlineplus/ency/article/002413.htm [Accessed 19 December 2011]

Miller, D. 2008. **Color Wheel of Fruits and Vegetables.** Disabled World [ONLINE] 12 January. Available at: http://www.disabled-world.com/artman/publish/fruits-vegetables.shtml [Accessed 5 February 2012]

Momtastic's Wholesome Baby Food. 2011. **Spice Up Your Baby's World – Learn about adding Spices and Herbs to Baby's Homemade Baby Foods.** [ONLINE] (Last updated on 26th July 2011). Available at: http://wholesomebabyfood.momtastic.com/tipspices.htm [Accessed 19 September 2011]

Natural Health Cure. 2011. **Health Benefits of Saffron.** [ONLINE] 2 March. Available at: http://www.naturalhealthcure.org/healing-medicinal-herbs/health-benefits-of-saffron-uses.html [Accessed 4 March 2012]

NHS Choices. 2011. **5 A DAY Portion Sizes.** [ONLINE] (Last reviewed on 6th December 2011). Available at: http://www.nhs.uk/Livewell/5ADAY/Pages/Portionsizes.aspx [Accessed 21 April 2012]

NHS Choices. **Milk and Dairy Foods.** [ONLINE] (Last reviewed on 15th March 2011). Available at: http://www.nhs.uk/livewell/goodfood/pages/milk-dairy-foods.aspx [Accessed 6 March 2012]

NHS Choices. 2011. **Understanding Food Groups.** [ONLINE] (Last reviewed on 29th July 2011). Available at: http://www.nhs.uk/Planners/birthtofive/Pages/Thefoodgroupsexplained.aspx [Accessed 16 March 2012]

NHS Choices. 2011. **Vitamins and Minerals – B Vitamins and Folic Acid.** [ONLINE] (Last reviewed on 14th March 2011). Available at: http://www.nhs.uk/Conditions/vitamins-minerals/Pages/Vitamin-B.aspx [Accessed 6 March 2012]

NHS Choices. 2011. **Vitamins and Minerals – Vitamin A.** [ONLINE] (Last reviewed on 14th March 2011) Available at: http://www.nhs.uk/CONDITIONS/VITAMINS-MINERALS/Pages/Vitamin-A.aspx [Accessed 6 March 2012]

NHS Choices. 2011. **Vitamins and Minerals – Vitamin K.** [ONLINE] (Last reviewed on 14th March 2011). Available at: http://www.nhs.uk/Conditions/vitamins-minerals/Pages/Vitamin-K.aspx [Accessed 7 March 2012]

NHS Choices. 2011. **Your Baby's First Solid Foods.** [ONLINE] (Last reviewed on 19th April 2011). Available at: http://www.nhs.uk/Conditions/pregnancy-and-baby/Pages/solid-foods-weaning.aspx [Accessed 13 August 2011]

Nutritional Supplements Centre. 2005. **Vitamin E.** [ONLINE] Available at: http://www.nutritionalsupplementscenter.com/info/vitamins/vitamine.html [Accessed 8 February 2012]

Schenker, S. 2010. **I've Heard Some Babies Are Allergic to Fruit. Which Fruits May Be A Problem?** Baby Centre, [ONLINE] Available at: http://www.babycentre.co.uk/baby/startingsolids/safety/fruit-allergy/ [Accessed 18 September 2011]

Teens Health. 2012. **Thyroid Disease and Teens.** [ONLINE] (Last reviewed February 2012). Available at: http://kidshealth.org/teen/diseases_conditions/growth/thyroid.html# [Accessed 4 March 2012]

The George Mateljan Foundation. 2001. **The World's Healthiest Foods – Avocados.** [ONLINE] Available at: http://www.whfoods.com/genpage.php?tname=foodspiceanddbid=5 [Accessed 24 November 2011]

The George Mateljan Foundation. 2001. **The World's Healthiest Foods –Cumin Seeds.** [ONLINE] Available at:http://www.whfoods.com/genpage.php?tname=foodspiceanddbid=91. [Accessed 11 January 2012]

The George Mateljan Foundation. 2001. **The World's Healthiest Foods – Garbanzo Beans.** [ONLINE] Available at: http://www.whfoods.com/genpage.php?tname=foodspiceanddbid=58 [Accessed 16 April 2012]

The George Mateljan Foundation. 2001. **The World's Healthiest Foods – Green Beans.** [ONLINE] Available at: http://www.whfoods.com/genpage.php?tname=foodspiceanddbid=134 [Accessed 30 September 2011]

The George Mateljan Foundation. 2001. **The World's Healthiest Foods – Onions.** [ONLINE] Available at: http://whfoods.org/genpage.php?dbid=45andtname=foodspice [Accessed 6 March 2012]

The George Mateljan Foundation. 2001. **The World's Healthiest Foods – Oregano.** [ONLINE] Available at: http://www.whfoods.com/genpage.php?tname=foodspiceanddbid=73 [Accessed 26 November 2011]

The George Mateljan Foundation. 2001. **The World's Healthiest Foods – Spinach.** [ONLINE] Available at: http://whfoods.org/genpage.php?tname=foodspiceanddbid=43 [Accessed 24 November 2011]

The George Mateljan Foundation. 2001. **The World's Healthiest Foods – Turmeric.** [ONLINE] Available at: http://whfoods.org/genpage.php?tname=foodspiceanddbid=78 [Accessed 2 October 2011]

Worden, J, GP. 2011. **Carbohydrates.** Net Doctor [ONLINE] (Last updated on 12th May 2011] Available at: http://www.netdoctor.co.uk/focus/nutrition/facts/lifestylemanagement/carbohydrates.htm [Accessed 28 February 2012]

Worden, J GP. 2011. **Protein.** Net Doctor [ONLINE] (Last updated on 23rd May 2011). Available at: http://www.netdoctor.co.uk/focus/nutrition/facts/detoxification/dietaryprotein.htm [Accessed 26 January 2012]

About the Author
Zainab Jagot Ahmed

Zainab is first-time mum to daughter Aaliyah, and currently resides in Leicester, England, with her husband and two cats. Prior to becoming a mummy, Zainab – a passionate home cook – worked in marketing in London for over 10 years in the fashion, entertainment and retail industries. And after the birth of her daughter, felt inspired to turn her attention to cooking nutrient-rich, homemade baby food. Zainab was keen to introduce Aaliyah to aromatic Asian flavours early when she began the weaning process, both to broaden Aaliyah's palate – allowing her to create lots of tasty meals without the use of salt or sugar and to introduce Aaliyah to her culinary heritage. However, she soon discovered there were no dedicated baby and toddler cookbooks with Asian or Asian-influenced recipes. After researching aromatic spices, dietary recommendations and various Super Foods, Zainab began inventing her own Indian-inspired baby-friendly meals, and soon friends were asking for recipes. Now she's giving everyone the chance to try them at home.

Keep up to date with the latest news and recipes from Zainab
Twitter: @ZainabJagAhmed
Facebook: facebook.com/ZainabJagotAhmed
www.ZainabJagotAhmed.com

Acknowledgements

This book is very special to me and I am hugely grateful to everyone who has helped me along this journey. Thank you to my original team of colleagues who helped me get to this point – Simon Maylott, Lee Smith, Greg Warner, Helen Lewis and Claire DeCiacco. This book wouldn't have been possible without your help and expertise. Double thanks to Simon Maylott for the introduction.

Special thanks to Sarfaraz Aziz of Photoshootr for the beautiful front cover photography and the original book design, and to baby sis Zaheera Iqbal for the great photography of yours truly inside the book.

Thanks to all the lovely folks over at Ebury who have worked really hard to make this edition possible, especially Rebecca Smart - thank you for the opportunity, Laura Higginson, Jessica Barnfield, Kealey Rigden and Claire Wharton. Big thanks to Smith & Gilmour for their updated design.

Thanks to my family, hubby Omar Ahmed for the support, encouragement, and for putting up with all the evening and weekend work. My parents, Kulsum and Haroon Jagot, sisters Zeenat and Zaheera, brother-in-laws Sham and Arif. This truly has been a family affair! Thank you for all your encouragement and help.

My most important thanks go to my reason for writing this book, my little princess, my daughter Aaliyah.

Thank you for the inspiration.

Zainab xx

10 9 8 7 6 5 4 3 2 1

Ebury Press, an imprint of Ebury Publishing,
20 Vauxhall Bridge Road,
London, SW1V 2SA

Ebury Press is part of the Penguin Random House group of companies
whose addresses can be found at global.penguinrandomhouse.com

Copyright © Zainab Jagot Ahmed 2016
Photography © Zainab Jagot Ahmed 2016
Cover photography © Photoshootr 2016

Zainab Jagot Ahmed has asserted her right to be identified as the author of
this Work in accordance with the Copyright, Designs and Patents Act 1988

First published by Sweet Juicy Lime in 2014.
This edition first published by Ebury Press in 2016.

Designed by DeCiacco Design.
This edition revised and updated by Smith & Gilmour.

www.penguin.co.uk

A CIP catalogue record for this book is available from the British Library

ISBN: 978 1 78503 345 2

Colour origination by Rhapsody Ltd London
Printed and bound in China by Toppan Leefung